WISDOM LITERATURE
and the
STRUCTURE OF PROVERBS

OTHER BOOKS BY T. A. PERRY

Art and Meaning in Berceo's "Vida de Santa Oria"

Léon Hébreu, *Dialogues d'amour:* Edition and Commentary

Erotic Spirituality: The Integrative Tradition from Leone Ebreo to John Donne

Santob de Carrión, *Proverbios morales:* A Critical Edition

The Moral Proverbs of Santob de Carrión: Jewish Wisdom in Christian Spain

Dialogues with Kohelet: The Book of Ecclesiastes (Translation and Commentary)

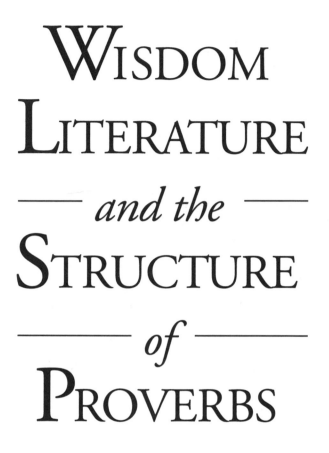

WISDOM LITERATURE

—— and the ——

STRUCTURE

—— of ——

PROVERBS

T. A. PERRY

THE PENNSYLVANIA STATE UNIVERSITY PRESS
UNIVERSITY PARK, PENNSYLVANIA

Library of Congress Cataloging-in-Publication Data

Perry, T. Anthony (Theodore Anthony), 1938–
    Wisdom literature and the structure of proverbs / T.A. Perry.
        p.   cm.
    Includes bibliographical references and index.
    ISBN 0-271-00929-2 (alk. paper)
    1. Wisdom literature—Criticism, literature, etc. 2. Proverbs
—History and criticism.   I. Title.
    BS1455.P43   1993
    398.9—dc20   92-33650
                                                                 CIP

Published by The Pennsylvania State University Press,
Barbara Building, Suite C, University Park, PA 16802-1003

It is the policy of The Pennsylvania State University Press to use acid-free paper for the
first printing of all clothbound books. Publications on uncoated stock satisfy the minimum
requirements of American National Standard for Information Sciences—Permanence of
Paper for Printed Library Materials, ANSI Z39.48–1984.

Avi,

שְׁמַע בְּנִי מוּסַר אָבִיךָ   וְאַל־תִּטֹּשׁ תּוֹרַת אִמֶּךָ :

Hear, my beloved son, the discipline of your Father,
And do not forsake the Torah of your Mother.

CONTENTS

PREFACE

Like bottles sculpted in bygone eras and cast upon the seas, proverbs survive the damages of time and carry messages of hidden treasure. Their very appearance is a challenge to the integrity of our containers: with what contempt would the milkman of my youth have viewed our modern plastic and disposable dispensers as against the noisier and heavier glass version with the cream on top! Strange enough, we long to drink from these time-capsules, as if their antiquated shapes and colors could magically transform our sour experience into the sweet liqueur of wisdom.

Some of these bottles have reached my doorstep, and I am first of all moved by the objects themselves, I want to study their ancient shapes, to speculate on their manufacture and original use. Yet is not to study some specimens to study them all? And is it of mere antiquarian interest to reflect upon the shapes of received things? I can imagine a cultural history, as imaginative as Lévi-Strauss's *The Raw and the Cooked,* that would study human mentality according to the history of its containers. Whether these bottles hold sweet cream or a still more precious substance can be known only from the tasting.

These pages study a fundamental structure of human thinking as exemplified in proverbial expression—the "containers" of my figure of speech. My hope is that, just as a bottle can clarify its contents, so to speak, the very shape of proverbs may tell us what they are about. This is not to argue that the bottle (or the form) is the message, but rather to pursue the more interesting question as to how structures can preserve and shape and transform their contents. The application to wisdom studies of such an approach is exciting, since from a study of the structure of wisdom we can perhaps glimpse the wisdom of structure.

This book is not a history of wisdom, either its literature or its ideology;

such a book would quite properly require careful attention to cultural moment and transformations, and at present "it is neither possible to write a chronological history of the development of wisdom literature nor to place each of the forms within its proper setting."[1] From such a historical perspective, for example, it would be unthinkable to speak in the same breath of the wisdom of Onchsheshonqy and La Rochefoucauld. Rather, I am concerned here with a single aspect of that tradition, though perhaps the most significant one: its understanding and creation and use of proverbs and its relation to other, preexistent proverbs, here termed "popular." It is thus, if you will, a book about proverbs, but from the perspective of an intellectual tradition, to use Whybray's (1974) important term, that thrived on their use and that contributed perhaps more than anyone to their proper understanding. It is hoped that the wisdom writers can afford us a glimpse into the essence of proverbial thinking and writing, and in so doing reveal something of their own intellectual enterprise.

This book thus aspires to serve as an introduction to wisdom literature, but in a special sense. A guru once remarked that to understand Saint Paul one would have to *be* Saint Paul—an adventure both noble and perhaps necessary, but one more likely to discourage understanding than advance it. In contrast to such a radical internalization but also to approaches external to the text such as history and sociology, I try to understand the wisdom tradition by (re)thinking its own thoughts, which may mean learning to think my own thoughts by using wisdom's recommended forms and structures of analysis. My approach assumes that wisdom can usefully be viewed as a specific tool of critical thinking and value analysis.

I write these pages as a student of literature and religion, joining the growing number of my colleagues who approach the Bible from a literary point of view and who therefore find interesting the parallels with the work of such scholars as Greimas and other structuralists, without necessarily sharing their enthusiasm for shop talk and jargon and metadiscourse.[2] Indeed, what student of proverbs writing today has not felt the enticement,

---

1. Crenshaw (1976, 22), who continues as follows: "Besides this inability to discern absolute dates and functions of the literature, it is impossible to write a history of the institution or persons responsible for compiling and transmitting the literature. Their origins are obscure, as is the overall development of the literature."

2. If only in the interest of readability, I shall make every effort to avoid the jargon current among both structuralists and their linguist mentors; the language is, I hope, plain English, with only unavoidable exceptions—such as "quadripartite"! You will thus search in vain for such gems as T–C (Topic-Comment) analysis or the herborized schemata of some linguistic diagrams, or discussion of *Tob-Sprüche* ("better-than" sayings). My own tastes gravitate toward the heuristic simplicity of medieval exegesis.

so characteristic of structuralists and students of semiotics and proverbs and wisdom literature alike, to discover the philosophers' stone, that fundamental, magical formula of signification or language or logic that can unlock the secrets of wisdom sayings? In the following pages I offer one such formula, derived not from the particularized discourse of modern theory (although clear parallels exist) but from the sages' own exegetical practice. My hope is that the transparency of their discourse will make wisdom proverbs more accessible by remaining as much as possible within the sages' world of discourse, and allowing students to think through proverbs from the inside, so to speak, by using wisdom's own structural models. By attempting to avoid both metatheory and discourse *about* discourse (two of the pitfalls of modern theory), I have thereby focused direct interest upon the sages' most enduring achievements: their finely crafted words and, along with that, their firm distrust of having the final word.

I am indebted to several friends and scholars for their many helpful suggestions, notably James L. Crenshaw, Carol Fontaine, David Jobling, Wolfgang Mieder, and Raymond C. Van Leeuwen. To my loving wife and children, my debt of gratitude has gone without saying for so long that it is time to acknowledge it here.

ABBREVIATIONS

Abot	Pirkei Abot [Ethics of The Fathers]
BP	*Libro de los buenos proverbios* (1879 edition)
BT	Babylonian Talmud
chap.	chapter (chaps. = chapters)
CSIC	Consejo Superior de Investigaciones Científicas
E	English, where numbering differs from MT
JSOT	*Journal for the Study of the Old Testament*
Koh	Kohelet
Kohelet	The Book of Ecclesiastes
Lucanor	Juan Manuel, *El conde Lucanor* (1983 edition)
MF	Honein Ibn Isaac, *Musrei ha-Filosofim*
MT	Massoretic Text (the standard Hebrew version)
n.	note
NJV	*Tanakh,* the new JPS translation of the Hebrew Bible
RSV	The Revised Standard Version of the Bible
Santob	Santob de Carrión, *Proverbios morales*
v.	verse (vv. = verses)

All references to the Bible and to classical texts give chapter followed by verse or appropriate subdivision. Thus, Abot 5:12 refers to Pirkei Abot, chapter 5, mishnah 12. All biblical and other translations are mine unless otherwise noted; translations from Kohelet are from my translation *Dialogues with Kohelet.* For the Mishnah I translate with a close eye to Danby's translation. All reference to Santob de Carrión is to my Spanish edition of the *Proverbios morales* (1986) and/or to my English translation (1987). Biblical books are abbreviated according to guidelines published in the *Journal of Biblical Literature* 107, no. 3 (September 1988): 579–96, except that Kohelet is Koh.

For the transliteration of Hebrew, since in all cases the goal is less to reproduce the exact spelling of MT than to recall the shape of the Hebrew words, vowels are transliterated as they would sound in an English reading. Consonants are transliterated as follows: ʾ *b g d h w z ḥ t y k l m n s ʿ p ts q r s sh t.*

INTRODUCTION[1]

1. Wisdom Sayings and Popular Proverbs:
Origins or Functions?

This book is about "wisdom" literature from the biblical period to the Renaissance. This focus is motivated
by a need to expand the range of vision practiced in
current research, which is typically intent on explain-
ing one of the Scriptures (Hebrew or Christian) by
parallels with antecedent traditions—and it must be
admitted that such parallels, while usually illuminating,
are rarely established as influences. This book is not
a history, however, but rather an attempt, by recon-
sidering classical texts in the light of different parallels
and models, to describe and understand what "the sages"
tried to achieve; it proceeds by focusing on a particular
aspect of their activity, their analysis and production
of proverbs and/or wisdom sayings. The sages were of
course masters of deeds as well as words, and yet it is
fair to say that it is mainly through their *words* that
they had—and continue to have—their chief impact.

---

1. A much earlier version of this Introduction appeared in *Proverbium* 4 (1987): 187–210, some of
the material of which has been reassigned in this study.

So too did their disciples view them, as "experts of [word] collections," and their *words* as "goads" to proper behavior.[2]

Proverbs were not only the sages' preferred mode of teaching but also a linguistic fact of life that formed an important part of their received cultural environment. Let us, for convenience, call these preexistent maxims "popular," referring in many cases to their origins and popularity among the folk. A German legal document of the fourteenth century expresses this popular love for maxims: "Whenever you can attach a proverb, do so, for the peasants like to judge according to proverbs" (A. Taylor 1931, 87). Such is also the case of the taunting of King Saul by what must have been a popular saying: "Is Saul too among the prophets?" (1 Sam 10:11, 12; 19:24).

Such harmony between popular proverb and learned literary discourse is not the rule, however, at least not in wisdom (con)texts, for sages were skeptical of the givens of proverb utterance, especially its presumption of authority, its rhetoric or *impression* of stating absolute truths. The distinction I have in mind, between popular proverbs and wisdom sayings, as well as the sages' critical approach to proverbial discourse, can be previewed by pondering the three following statements:

1. Better dead than red.
2. Consider well the proportions of things: It is better to be a young June-bug than an old bird of paradise. (Mark Twain, *Pudd'nhead Wilson's Calendar*)
3. There are four types of almsgivers: he that is minded to give but not that others should give—he is stingy with what belongs to others; he that is minded that others should give but not that he should give—he is stingy with what belongs to himself; he that is minded to give and also that others should give—he is a saintly man; he that is minded not to give and that others should not give—he is a wicked man. (Abot 5:13)[3]

Stylistically, the first is the more proverbial-sounding of the lot, mainly because of its brevity and rhyme. Yet this "popular" surface highlights both its tremendous power and its danger, its great "popularity" in its day but also its easy alliance with stereotype and sloganeering. One would easily label it a popular proverb, except that its author happens to be known (Senator Joseph McCarthy). The third, by contrast, despite its highly formulaic surface, or

---

2. Koh 12:11, where *dibrei* has its frequent ambiguity, referring to "words" but also to "deeds."
3. For the wider literary context of this text, see the Appendix.

perhaps because of it, is concerned primarily with thinking over simple assertion, with evaluation or graded distinctions of value as well as valuation. I would wager that it has never enjoyed great popularity, except in rather restricted circles, yet its *method* of thinking has been crucial to civilized values. Between the two stands the familiar compromise, the historical "better-than" saying, which attempts to synthesize the merits of the other two, the slick brevity of the first and the analytic discursiveness of the third; it does so by the characteristic "wisdom" focus on reflection: "consider well!"

I shall first argue that, despite obvious formal or stylistic differences, all three statements are comparable at a deeper level and thus, *structurally* speaking, can fruitfully be analyzed by a logical structure that I call "quadripartite," here modeled by the Abot text. Recent research has brought into clearer focus the logical structures and formulas inherent in proverbs, but I shall show that similar structures have been consciously used for centuries in the production of proverbs and in the analysis of the values they express. For example, Juan Manuel (Spain, fourteenth century), the famous author of *El conde Lucanor,* wrote the following "proverb" in his collection of maxims that concludes that work:

> All things
> appear good and are good,
> and appear bad and are bad,
> and appear good and are bad,
> and appear bad and are good.

In so doing he was not only proposing a conundrum rather typical of his aphoristic method but also, I would suspect, extending an invitation similar to the Abot text to reflect on the structure of sayings in general. Such structural awareness, based on ancient methods and made more theoretically explicit through the quadripartite model, amounts to a rather new way of thinking about proverbs, allows comparison of proverbs from very different historical periods and situations, and adds a mode of analysis to the study of individual sayings. Such is the burden of this book.

In making the distinction between "proverbs" and "wisdom sayings," I am of course aware that "proverbs" can refer to learned as well as popular adages: Do we not have the biblical Book of Proverbs, composed mainly of learned sayings? Moreover, the difficulty of such distinctions can be seen in texts such as Proverbs 1–9, where the opposing ideologies, personified as Dame Wis-

dom and the Foreign Woman, both use proverbs and even identical language
(Yee 1989)! It may be that the decisive distinction between the two, as
exemplified by the McCarthy and Abot examples above, has to do less with
"origins" such as social ideologies (popular vs. aristocratic) or *Sitz im Leben*
(folk vs. academy) or modes of transmission (oral vs. written) than with the
degree to which structure is concealed (in the first case) or displayed and
exploited, as in the Abot and *Lucanor* texts. The crucial distinction I have in
mind resides in the fact that among its practitioners "wisdom" sayings or
proverbs imply a critical stance, a deliberate distancing from worldly wisdom.[4]
From this perspective, the Foreign Woman's monologic assertion that "stolen
water is sweet" (Prov 9:17) is a "popular" proverb (whether it achieved
"popularity" and had "currency among the folk" is undocumented, as is
usually the case) and occasions Wisdom's rebuttal. In brief, "wisdom" is used
here less to indicate origins than a set of (structural) functions and (intellectual)
values, and its natural enemy would be "popular" proverbs, those that take
the assumed stance of popularity, of authoritarian or majority truths. Moreover,
there seems to be a developing consensus regarding the importance of such
an approach, "since the problems which occur in the study of all types of
sayings are fundamentally the same, regardless of the origin of [the] saying"
(Fontaine 1982, 179 n. 43).

The distinction between proverbs and (the critical stance of) wisdom
proverbs is not true of all wisdom, but it does in part characterize Kohelet
(third century B.C.E.?), Abot (around the second century C.E.), Honein
(ninth century), and Juan Manuel (fourteenth century). A tradition spanning
nearly two millenia is certainly significant and, especially given its self-
reflective tendency, important for its insights into wisdom itself. It may well
be the case that such cross-comparisons become possible not only because the
basic presuppositions of language do not change (e.g., the natural tendency
to perceive linguistic oppositions) but because the basic structures of proverbs are extremely stable and conservative. This stability itself is of course
related to ideology, as I discuss in Chapter 3, but I wish to stress a more
stylistic and structural continuum. How can it be, for example, that two
complexly structured proverbs at a thousand years' distance could sound
exactly the same, that Juan Manuel can end up sounding exactly like Abot?

Assuming the distinction between wisdom and nonwisdom sayings or

---

4. From wisdom's function to be critical, it follows not only that it must be always watchful but
also that it cannot be systematically antagonistic; this accounts for a number of approving uses of
popular proverbs ("as the people say") in classical wisdom texts such as those found in the Bible or the
Talmud or Spanish texts such as *Lucanor*.

proverbs, I am particularly interested in how a group of people, let us call them sages or scholars, in their awareness of the tremendous power of proverbs, developed safeguards for their use and articulated them for their own purposes. Thus, "wisdom" in this sense is deliberately "anti" something, but obviously not necessarily against the use of proverbs. In my attempt to develop new perspectives for the study of proverbs and wisdom literature, I shall of course be interested in what modern research and theory has to say, notably structuralism. Yet my primary focus will be on authors historically closer to the original biblical texts and more existentially involved with the wisdom enterprise. Thus, in my study of the Anchos legend, I ask how one sage (or his "collector," i.e., preserver and commentator) viewed the origin and meaning of proverbs. My purpose here is to shift critical attention away from both source-hunting and structure and to try to describe how the wisdom process was understood by its devotees, and in particular how wisdom values must function in a world and environment that uses proverbs, especially what I call proverbs of simple preference.

2. Structure, Form, and Content

Wisdom has built her house, she has fashioned [RSV: set up] her seven pillars.

—Prov 9:1

It is an error, I feel, to see a literary work as having only two layers: one of form and one of content. Form itself is made up of several levels: structure is one of these.

—Barthes (1972, 77)

It would be interesting to assess the extent to which the Aristotelian notions of form and matter once dominated a certain level of literary analysis as style and content. French studies in particular, perhaps because they are more prone to theory and conceptual routing, have stressed the partition of texts into *forme et fond,* viewing each text as a mixture of the two and dividing up the entire history of literature according to the dosage of allegiance to one or the other. Even Barthes's attempt to expand the formula in fact reduces structure to being a level of form. In the United States academic criticism still feels the tug of the New Criticism of the 1950s and 1960s, with its fine but exclusive focus on the text and especially the "poem itself."

In such a division of literary empire, proverbs can easily be assigned to the "content" end of the spectrum, since they purport to deliver an all-important message. Yet, the fact that proverbs are easily recognizable suggests that formal devices are equally decisive. Thus, in biblical criticism, for example, interest in Hebrew wisdom has focused primarily on the message, fluctuating narrowly, it is true, between wisdom's debt to earlier school or courtly traditions and its existence as autonomous teaching. Yet, since a proverb's meaning is made more effective through a wide range of stylistic enhancements, form analysis has been recognized as an important adjunct of such studies. As William McKane aptly put it (1970, 267), "wisdom embraces form as well as content, and it matters that what is said should be said well and elegantly. The wise man is the master of compressed, polished epigrammatic utterance." With the rapidly accelerating rapprochement between biblical and literary critics, prospects are good that textual studies of the wisdom canon will progress further in the direction of rhetoric and other formalistic concerns.

One such concern among biblical critics—parallelism or the rhetorical balancing of synonymous phrases and thoughts—has been considered as one of the most popular witnesses to the wisdom writers' enduring concern for form as well as substance. Yet there is at least one important school of exegetes, the Rabbis, that strenuously denies the purely stylistic understanding of such techniques, insisting that in the Bible there is no such thing as repetition and that such formalistic devices are but occasions for the exploration of new meanings and different applications (Kugel 1981, 96–103). As expressed in the Talmud, "several meanings may issue from a single verse, but one meaning may not issue from two different verses" (BT Sanhedrin 33b). Such a concept, based on the polysemic character of the Torah (Faur 1986, xiii), certainly increases the subservience of literary form to content, and it does so by viewing style as a further means of expanding meaning and interpretation. The Rabbinic notion of parallelistic form is the opposite of a stricture, however, since it imposes a generative imperative on the interpretation of verse structure.

The relation between form and meaning is thus far from simple, and the view that style is but an elegant enhancement may produce more confusion than it dispels, by diverting attention from those deeper levels of form— what I shall refer to as structure—that *produce* meaning. Contrary to the usual notion that meaning always precedes form both logically and chronologically, one researcher senses that wisdom aphorisms "often seem to originate in the desire to experiment with a linguistic formula" (Battesti 1974, 4). And just as too strong a focus on stylistics may be counterproductive at the level of composition, so too in interpretation. It has been observed that similar stylistic traits may actually conceal different logical structures and thus obstruct the analysis of meaning (Permyakov 1979, 178).

Form and content hardly exhaust the horizon of study, therefore, and there is a growing awareness of a third area, that of structure, that can appear to overlap with the other two but that is quite distinct. The concept can be previewed at a quite simple level. Take, for example, the wisdom writers' frequent use of number and numerical patterns such as they occur in biblical composition (see Roth 1965) and in early Rabbinic writing (Wünsche 1911, 1912). It is not uncommon for such a phenomenon to occur in "strings," such as the following well-known formula:

> *Three* things are never satisfied; *four* never say "enough" . . .
>
> *Three* things are too wonderful for me; *four* I do not understand, etc. (Prov 30:15–31)

Such techniques facilitated memorization, thus strengthening the proverb's didactic utility, and they also provided collectors with convenient tags for classifying and organizing their materials. However, numerical patterns also exerted their influence at the compositional level, as incentives to round out and complete a formula by coming up with further examples. In this respect the number to be reached has a function analogous to that of poetic meter or form such as the sonnet, where the poet's striving to complete the mandatory fourteen lines is similar to the wisdom writer's invention of additional elements in order to complete the pattern. Indeed, as the author's efforts become directed to adjusting the components to fit the requirements of the patterns (Zakovitch 1977), such numerical formulas rapidly become literary structures in their own right, used not only to beautify and order but also to organize and expand individual units and entire sections. Thus, just as parallelism blurs the rigid distinction between form and content, numerical composition points beyond purely surface literary form to compositional patterns. And just as writers had fixed formulas of composition, it may be that sages had formulas to guide or provoke their thinking. The first are now being studied in the flourishing field of rhetoric; the second can profitably be analyzed through structural studies.

It appears necessary, then, to investigate the notion of structure and its relation to meaning. As G. L. Permyakov, the great pioneer in such research, has shown (1979, 179), it seems beyond doubt that the most fruitful approach to a general theory of the proverbial genre is "the treatment of proverbial sayings as semiotic units within the system of the logical transformations thereof." The limits of this approach cannot be predicted at present, but Kuusi (1972b, 735) perceives a growing consensus that even if "structural analysis is not the skeleton key to all the locked doors of paremiology . . . , it is a key that opens the way from seeming equivalences and differences to an ordered perception of essential similarities and contrasts." A program for such an enterprise was in fact outlined by Barthes (1970, 107), who also noted its special relevance for the study of proverbs:

> What is easy for proverbs (whose syntactic and archaising form is quite special) is much less the case for other codes of discourse, since the phrastic model, the example, the paradigm has not (yet) been described. One can nevertheless imagine that stylistics, which until now has been preoccupied only with . . . authors' idiolects, will radically change its orientation and focus on defining and classifying models (patterns) of sentences, clausulas, cadences, armatures, deep structures; in a word, stylistics could in turn become transformational . . .

It would be well to say, first of all, what my understanding of structure is not. Just as it is distinct from form and meaning, structure is not to be confused with those "spiritual structures" that are a work's main theme and that constitute its deepest life-questions, as Zimmerli has used the term in a famous article (1933). Structure does of course have a primary relation to one's ideology and worldview, but this relation is general rather than specific; it asserts the very possibility of ideology by positing that the primary aspect of proverbs is valuational (see Chapter 3.2).

A second and more tempting form of totalization must also be avoided: the ambition to reduce all linguistic data to a single structure. Rather than searching for *one* structure, I have assumed, while isolating and focusing upon a single structure, that other such structures exist and can be subject to similar investigations. This was indeed the structuralists' ambition, of Lévi-Strauss, for instance, as described by Genette (1966, 99), who "refused to search out the structure of a global society and more prudently sought some structures, wherever they are, without claiming that everything is structurable." Thus, while arguing that the quadripartite is both historically and theoretically important, I use it mainly heuristically, as one interesting approach to the understanding of proverbs, albeit a necessary element in the analysis of what I call "wisdom" sayings.

Another popular use of "structure" is that proposed by Todorov (1970, 100): "The distinction between form and content must be transcended. . . . This is indeed one of the purposes of the concept of structure: to transcend the old dichotomy between form and content in order to conceive of the work as a dynamic totality and unity." This notion will be avoided here because my interest is not in literary criticism as such (as understood by Todorov), that is to say, not in the interpretation of specific works of literature. My focus, rather, is closer to the notion of structure presented by Todorov in another context (1970, 48–51), that of poetics or the description of configurations or paradigms that can invade any number of works and genres—although, in practice, such structures flourish in their greatest intensity and concentration in wisdom collections such as the Book of Proverbs.

In this study *structure* is viewed primarily as a way to manage meaning, to analyze, generate one from another, and evaluate proverbial propositions by applying the appropriate formulas. In particular, two types of propositions are examined in detail: "better-than" proverbs such as "better dead than red," and equational proverbs such as "business is business." It is the case, however, that whereas purely literary forms are easily spotted, wisdom proverbs occur in a variety of patterns and reveal their complete identity only through analysis, which in this case involves their being related to a relevant deep structure. In wisdom proverbs, what I call the quadripartite structure—four parts or propositions are always implied—seems to be one of the keys of proverbial construction. My purpose in Chapter 1 will be to isolate and describe this basic structure as it actually occurs in proverbs and to analyze its transformational and interpretative properties. With this heuristic model firmly in mind, Chapter 2 will present some of the forms of wisdom, some of its main stylistic variants and generative possibilities. Though my examples do not claim to exhaust the vast and varied domain of proverbial discourse, it should become possible to project the implications of this research for the study of proverbs in general at both structural and formal levels. Thus, in Chapter 3 wisdom structures are considered as content, not in any exhaustive and historical way but as relates to the structural studies presented here. To put the matter differently, I shall ask what the historical existence of quadripartite structures can teach us about the wisdom enterprise itself. Chapter 4 departs somewhat from the purely structural focus and, again working from historical rather than modern theoretical models, focuses on wisdom's themes, especially those that have emerged in this study.

My focus in Chapter 1 on the "context-free kernel," which has been called the sense as opposed to the referent (Camp 1985, 180), carries two dangers. On the one hand, in trying to see through or beyond the blandishments of style to the deeper structures, I may properly be suspected of disregarding the importance of style and, indeed, the particular meaning of individual sayings; on the other, my initial focus on the pure forms and logical relations inherent in sayings makes abstraction of historicity and real-life context. In response to the first objection, in Chapter 2 I attempt to show the interplay of deep structure and many of its formulaic and stylistic metamorphoses; this attempt is in some respects akin to rhetorical or "form-critical" or "architectural" formulas. In Chapter 3, I address the second objection and, by studying the differences of intellectual orientation between simple and complex sayings, try to assess whether form (the uses of certain structures and styles) can yield any clues about the possible functions of wisdom in daily life. Admittedly, the relation of "real life" to literature is not a simple one, and it seems rather ambitious to wish to gather sociology from literary texts by applying the findings of structural study "in its literary setting *and in society as well*" (Fontaine 1982, 26). For the moment, at least, I shall focus only on how real life is projected by the wisdom literary context.[5] In this spirit, Chapter 4 gives a rather moving example from the wisdom tradition itself of how that tradition represented a real-life setting in which the creation of wisdom sayings is seen to occur.

It is best to try to anticipate any mistaken impressions that such an approach may produce. In this study I focus on an important and neglected aspect of wisdom literature, an approach with both historical precedent and parallels in contemporary critical models. The sages' interest in structure seems clear and central; indeed, it was part and parcel of their commitment to what would today be called critical thinking. But this focus does not deny the sages' religious commitment and replace their faith by logic. Indeed, sages of all ages manifested a clear commitment to a set of values, here called wisdom as opposed to worldly values, and their values were typically what would be termed today "religious." But it may also be the case that their interest in structure can in fact be considered as one of those wisdom values.

---

5. The distinctions outlined above have recently been applied to wisdom texts by Van Leeuwen (1988, 23). With reference to Bryce's study of Prov 25:2–27, he remarks that "his analysis of form and content remains on the level of 'surface' structures and does not attempt to lay bare the 'deep' structures which contribute to the 'meaning effect' of the passage."

3. The Literary and Structural Study of Wisdom Sayings

Despite recent advances in proverb research and wisdom studies (mostly biblical), each seems content to pursue its separate ways. The reasons for this state of affairs are deeply ingrained and partially justified. Is there not, at the top of the list, a crucial distinction between popular traditions and learned ones; the former are held to be democratic and universalist, while wisdom texts are often thought to have originated among the elite and at court? In addition to social ideology there is also the nature of transmission: folklore is conveyed orally, whereas wisdom survives in texts and compositions of a highly literary nature. Thus it is that folkloric proverbs continue to be collected, but it is rare when new manuscripts turn up of ancient wisdom.[6] And just as literary considerations rank rather low among the interests of folklorists and paremiologists, biblical scholars scrutinize the meaning of their texts with the help of philology and theology but rarely in terms of the (logical and literary) forms of composition and transmission.

There are notable exceptions, however. I have mentioned above the growing trend to study the "Bible as literature," and such scholars as Roland Murphy, author of an excellent form-critical survey of the biblical wisdom corpus, has recently acknowledged the need for more study of the rhetorical dimension of these texts (1981, xiii). In biblical studies one need think only of the work of Carol Fontaine, Claudia Camp, and Raymond C. Van Leeuwen, especially geared to the study of structure as it is understood here. Most notable is David Jobling's and Daniel Patte's applications of structural models to biblical narrative and metaphor (for an example of the latter, see Chapter 1.2). Such study is just beginning, however, and its medieval antecedents in such scholars as Menachem ha-Meiri need to be further explored. In addition, the results of the two camps of researchers require further integration: first, the growing interest in the rhetoric of wisdom texts by such scholars as Murphy and Crenshaw; second, the increasingly sophisticated structural approaches to paremiology by such scholars as Milner, Dundes, Permyakov, and Grzybek, to name but a few.

---

6. Rare but not impossible; witness the rapidly expanding corpus of Mesopotamian wisdom and their publication by such scholars as Bendt Alster and William W. Hallo.

4. Proof-Texts: The Bible, the Rabbis, and Medieval Spain

From my hypothesis of universally applicable structures, it follows that proof-texts can and must come from everywhere and anywhere, oral as well as written, learned but also popular. This is consistent with the international and intercultural character of both proverbs and wisdom literature.[7] Nevertheless, in my selection I have favored — but not exclusively — several kinds of texts. On the one hand, I apply my method to those highly standard texts from Scripture that are universally known and thus have quite understandably been the focus of much interest, notably Proverbs, Kohelet (Ecclesiastes), and the Wisdom of Ben Sirach. On the other hand, it needs to be considered that Wisdom is an ongoing tradition extending from the prebiblical period to modern times and with notable points of transmission. An area of great interest in this regard is medieval Spain, where there was an extraordinary flowering of the genre of proverbs and, perhaps for that reason, historical texts that self-consciously exhibit theoretical interest in their subject. There is also cultural interest in such a selection, since in Spain Christians, Muslims, and Jews interacted and flourished side by side to a degree unknown in the rest of Europe. Indeed, Spain's oriental communities claimed to represent, beyond their own rich traditions, the wisdom of the ancient world.[8] Because of these contacts, Spain was in a unique position both to receive and also to transmit. While thus hosting a synthesis and summation of previous wisdom traditions, Spain also provided a fresh point of departure, a primary source of wisdom literature for further elaboration in Western culture. There would seem to be a need, therefore, to make some of these materials better known to scholars.[9]

Three highly representative medieval wisdom collections have been espe-

7. V. P. Anikin, in his "Theses on the International and National Study of Proverbs," makes this connection quite clearly: "The study of the typological commonness and similarity of proverbs of different peoples aims at the elucidation of the *logical formulae and figures* which are contained in proverbial utterances" (quoted in Grzybek 1987, 45).

8. F. Rosenthal (1940, 394) points out that in the Islamic world "it may have happened that an author added Plato's name only for ornament . . . , but such a supposition must be considered as a last expedient."

9. There is no full-length study of wisdom in medieval Spain, and a more extensive treatment of this major corpus must await my forthcoming monograph. Here I can only list a number of these highly interesting collections: the *Bocados de oro, Calila y Dimna, Castigos y documentos para bien vivir,* Petrus Alfonsi's *Disciplina Clericalis, Flores de filosofía, Libro de Alexandre,* Juan Manuel's *El conde Lucanor, Libro de Apolonio, Libro de los buenos proverbios, El Libro del cauallero Zifar, Libro de los cien capítulos, Libro de los exenplos por a. b. c.,* Santob de Carrión's *Proverbios morales,* to mention only the better-known ones in Old Spanish. The entire corpus deserves to be better known and studied, especially in relation to Arabic and Hebrew sources and points of transmission.

cially helpful. Toward the middle of the ninth century the Coptic Christian physician Honein Ibn Isaac, the celebrated translator of Greek scientific treatises into Arabic, set his mind to collecting the wisdom and sayings of the sages of Greek antiquity in order to preserve them for posterity. The text of this remarkably long and rich anthology of proverbs remains unedited to this day in its Arabic original, but two translations continue to be available: the anonymous thirteenth-century Spanish *Libro de los buenos proverbios,* and the *Musrei ha-Filosofim,* which is the Hebrew translation by the important Hispano-Jewish poet Al-Harizi (1170–1235).[10] The second major proverb collection from Spain that has served this study is that of Juan Manuel (1282–1349?), nephew of King Alfonso X (the Wise) and author of a collection of tales after the manner of Petrus Alfonsi's *Disciplina Clericalis,* the extraordinary *Book of Patronio, or Count Lucanor.* The work groups fifty tales, each summarized by a proverb,[11] and the author then appends an additional 180 original proverbs, written in a style that betrays the influences of the ongoing wisdom tradition. Due to Juan Manuel's enduring popularity in Spain, his *Count Lucanor* has been the subject of numerous studies, but his work in proverbs unjustly continues to be neglected.[12] Third, I continue to be enriched by the study of that remarkable intellectual autobiography in proverbs, Rabbi Santob de Carrión's *Moral Proverbs,* strongly influenced by Christian and Arabic as well as Jewish wisdom (cf. Perry 1987b).

The critical presuppositions of my method require comment. Intertextuality, variously interpreted and practiced especially by Bible scholars, has played an important role in wisdom study. The Ancient Near Eastern context has furnished, if not sources or influences, as least parallels and useful points of comparison. But study has not proceeded in both chronological directions, and the comparative method could usefully be expanded to include later as well as earlier texts. Of particular interest is the ongoing tradition of wisdom texts just mentioned, which thrived until at least the end of the Middle Ages. Mishnaic sages, medieval collectors, and authors of sayings—all were con-

10. In this study I translate from the Hebrew version of Al-Harizi, but with help from the better-known Spanish text when the meaning is unclear. The text consists of a collection of proverbs of antiquity (5–36 in the Old Spanish version), followed by wise sayings inspired by the life and especially the death of Alexander the Great (37–59; see Plessner 1954–55, 60–61). There is also a German translation of Al-Harizi's text by Loewenthal (Honein 1896b).

11. For the relation between tale and proverb, see Perry (1987a).

12. Juan Manuel's proverb collection has been characterized by Sturken (1974, 100) as "some of the most mind-dulling pages that Juan Manuel ever wrote." Barry Paul Taylor's (1983) highly interesting study of these proverbs suggests a different view and will, I hope, orient future research in more productive directions. The best introduction to the *Count Lucanor* remains Daniel Devoto's astonishing bibliographical essay (1972).

scious continuators, and their words are therefore important as applications and interpretations of earlier traditions. They often voiced similar preoccupations; their writings echoed the same assumptions and sought to reproduce identical structures. In judging texts by later developments there are dangers of anachronism, of course: the extreme example of this being Barthes's *S/Z*, which, by appending Balzac's text as an annex to his own commentary on that story, reverses chronological logic by suggesting that Balzac is really a commentary on Barthes! However, such dangers must be balanced by the possibility that traditions are organic unities, that later texts can develop and thus clarify as well as distort the meaning of earlier contributions.[13] This possibility also implies the requirement to study medieval criticism—among my favorites are Rabbi Menachem ha-Meiri's (d. 1316) theories of proverb organization in the Book of Proverbs. As an example of the value of medieval wisdom collections as commentaries on the continuing tradition, I study in Chapter 4 "The Cranes of Ibycus" story as a conscious parable of earlier, wisdom views on the origins and nature of proverbs.

In addressing itself primarily to texts common to the "Judeo-Christian" tradition from the Book of Proverbs through the fifteenth century, this study thus invokes the spokesmen and exegetes of those traditions in an attempt to clarify cultural values and differences. However, since my historical texts function primarily as material for structural analyses, they can then be applied to other value systems. In other words, the exegetical and historical components of this study should not be allowed to camouflage the transcultural importance of the structures themselves. Indeed, it is hoped that future research will address the question as to precisely what extent the quadripartite in particular is applicable to other value systems. This would not be inconsistent with the wisdom writers' persuasion that wisdom is an intercultural genre and that its structures are constitutive of thought itself.[14] At the very least, however, I hope to reexamine samples of the biblical and wisdom corpus from a new perspective, to expand the possibilities of reading and thinking about proverbs.

---

13. This shortcoming mars the otherwise interesting study on the sage edited by Gammie and Perdue (1990), which examines the topic from the remotest origins but rather arbitrarily stops around the second century C.E., although the wisdom tradition—the intellectual environment that had recognizable "sages"—continued until the end of the Middle Ages.

14. "Wisdom is the form of the intelligence (*tsurat ha-sekel*)" (*MF:*7); "la sapiencia es forma del seso" (*BP:*8; cf. also Prov 9:1).

1

THE STRUCTURE OF WISDOM
Quadripartite Models

1. The Historical Quadripartite

Marguerite de Navarre, author of the riotous *Heptaméron* (sixteenth century), tells the well-known tale of a lover, reputedly her brother King François I of France, who, in order to reach the bedroom of his beloved, had to pass by a monastery (tale 25). The point of the story is not the adultery itself but rather the King's great religious devotion, since he never failed to linger in prayer at the monastery after leaving his mistress' arms. Now, whether the moral of the story be the King's devotion or his hypocrisy, both readings would notice the paradoxical nature of man and the inconsistencies of his behavior.

Behavioral contradictions have been noted by moralists in all ages, but the literary mode of presentation and exploration has taken different forms. The following tale or *ma'aseh* becomes verbal only in its interpretive phase, and its moral point is aggressively paradoxical:

> Once upon a time there was a great drought, and the Jews were anxious for rain, so the rabbis sent to

Hilkiah to ask him to pray for rain. When the two rabbis came to his house, they did not find him in, so they went out to the field to look for him. They found him in a vineyard, where he was removing the weeds to prevent their further growth. They greeted him with the words: "The Lord be with you," but he did not even turn his face to them . . .

[Later] they said to him: "When we greeted you the first time, why did you not pay any attention to us?" He replied: "I was hired to work by the day and could not spare the time to speak to you." (Gaster 1934, 151–53)

The pedagogical point of the story is that politeness (exemplifying a worldly value [**w**]) has no force and must be completely suspended in the context of a wisdom value (**W**) such as honesty. Or, more precisely, honest impoliteness is "better than" dishonest politeness.

At times such a structural analysis becomes more explicit, especially in exegesis, which seems to have been regarded as a congenial environment. To a Jewish midrashist of the third century, for example, the most appropriate occasion for taking notice of behavioral paradoxes might be a scriptural difficulty, such as the one raised by Isa 3:10: "Say of the righteous, *when he is good,* that they shall eat the fruits of their deeds."[1] What, asked the midrashist, can the italicized attribute possibly describe?

Is there a righteous man who is good and a righteous man who is not good! Rather, one who is good towards Heaven and good towards his fellow man, he is a good righteous person; [but] one who is good towards Heaven and bad towards his fellow man, he is a righteous man who is not good. Similarly, you read: "Woe unto the evil wicked man, for the reward of his hands shall be done unto him" (Isa 3:11). But is there a wicked man who is evil and one who is not evil! Rather, one who is evil towards Heaven and evil towards his fellow man, he is [called] evil wicked; but one who is evil toward Heaven but not evil toward his fellow man, he is called a wicked man who is not evil. (BT Qiddushin 40a)

From the simple noun and attribute, or rather from the two values "righteous" and "good," four distinct levels of behavior have been inferred. These are,

1. This translation interprets the Hebrew *ki tob* as "*when* he is good." RSV interprets *ki* as the relative: "Tell the righteous *that* it shall be well with them, for they shall eat the fruit of their deeds."

restated in a paradigmatic form that will be explained later (the "+" indicates positive value and the "−" indicates negative value):

1. righteous and good $(++)$
2. righteous and not good $(+-)$
3. not righteous and good $(-+)$
4. not righteous and not good $(--)$

One of the intriguing grounds for cultural debate in such a paradigm can be focused on the logical connective "and": whether it is causal (good "because" righteous) or simply conjunctive (good "and" righteous). Religious people might propose a bond of causality between the topics in propositions 1 and 4, arguing that religion leads to ethical behavior and that "the fool who says in his heart" that there is no God (Ps 53:1) will also behave unethically. But the same people might reject causality in the intermediate propositions 2 and 3, which observe that atheists can behave morally and even, paradoxically, that people with a highly refined sense of religiosity can commit unethical actions. In the above passage, for example, "the Rabbis here use the terms 'wicked' (*rasha*) and 'righteous' (*tsaddiq*) in the technical sense of what we would today call a man with religious feeling" (Jacobs 1978, 47). The values attributed to each behavioral type would of course vary according to culture and sensitivity.

The affinity between such a structural analysis and exegesis should be carefully noted, as well as its remarkable persistence, at least in Jewish exegesis. One further example must suffice. Consider how Malbim (Meir Loeb ben Jehiel Michael, nineteenth century), basing himself on Rabbinic tradition, interprets the opening verses of Jeremiah. As is frequently the case in traditional Jewish historiography, the purpose is to assess the impact of morality on the community's well being,

> In the days of Josiah the son of Amon (Jer 1:2): both he and his generation were righteous. . . . In the days of Jehoiakim (1:3): At that time the generation was righteous and the king was wicked, as the Sages said. Until the end of the eleventh year of Zedekia: For then the stature was reversed, for they were wicked and, by contrast, the king was righteous.

Here the slide from well-being to destruction is ascribed to an erosion of righteousness, which begins with the leadership and passes to the people of the next generation. Thus:

1. righteous king and righteous people = prosperity
2. wicked king and righteous people
3. righteous king and wicked people

The fourth and final stage, "wicked king and wicked people," the only remaining logical possibility and thus easily deduced from the existing terms, is left unexpressed because it is as obvious to the commentator (let us say that it is *logically* obvious) as it is inexpressible, since it would imply utter destruction. Such an ellipsis of one of the propositions gives a foretaste of more typical analyses. This particular structure also expresses an interesting better-than comparison: a righteous people, even with a wicked king, is better (safer from destruction) than a wicked people with a righteous king.

For the moment, however, the focus is not cultural values but rather the structure itself, a typical form of analysis of these values. One would hesitate to consider the Qiddushin text as a "wisdom proverb," despite the formulaic "as the sages said," at least not in the form typical of such collections as the Book of Proverbs, where there is a certain rule of brevity. But neither should one conclude that this characteristic form of value analysis is based on exegetical practice alone or even operates exclusively within that discipline. For there exists a historical corpus of such texts in what may be called their pure or "quadripartite" form. I shall first present these "proverbs" or wisdom sayings and then argue that they offer important insight into how proverbs function and how, through them, the sages analyzed cultural values.

Perhaps the best opportunity to note such elaborate sayings in their purity and variety occurs in chapter 5 of the Mishnah of Abot. Since presentation of the entire string would be distracting at this point, I shall extract a single saying from the Abot text and reproduce the remainder in the Appendix, along with a brief commentary. In these remarkable experiments the structure is fully given and the requirement is merely to isolate the better-than component. Even this is facilitated, however, by the presence of the "best" and the "worst." Note, too, that each valuational category includes a commentary cast in such a lapidary form as to become part of the maxim.

> There are four types among men: he that says, "What is mine is mine and what is yours is yours"—this is the common type, and some say that this is the type of Sodom; he that says, "What is mine is yours and what is yours is mine"—he is an ignorant man; he that says, "What is mine is yours and what is yours is your own"—he is a saintly man; and

he that says, "What is yours is mine, and what is mine is my own"—he is a wicked man. (Abot 5:10)

This text is explicitly structured according to the four possible combinations of two complementary terms or topics (and their opposites), one positive (give) and one negative (take):

I	II	III
1. doesn't give and doesn't take	(− +)	common type
2. gives and takes	(+ −)	ignorant man
3. gives and doesn't take	(+ +)	saintly man
4. doesn't give and takes	(− −)	wicked man

Ideologically speaking, we are again fortunate that the valuations have been included by the spokesman for the culture, here listed in column III. Thus, the plus and minus signs not only indicate oppositional topics but actually correspond to positive and negative values (thus, within the total structure these signs have both structural and semantic or moral value). In accord with the assigned values, this structure agrees with its well-known semantic variant: "It is better to give than to receive," since in statement 2 giving has positive value and taking has negative value. However, this does not imply that "giving" as a category of behavior is more highly valued than not "taking" or receiving, since statement 1 is considered as better than statement 2 in view of the high value that Jewish culture places on independence from others.[2] That is to say, rather surprisingly, that it is better not to take than to give. However, the commentary offers a second interpretation of proposition 1, insisting on the wickedness of one who refuses normal human exchange. This alternate view departs from the structural suggestions, and it seems to do so by interpreting the conjunctive as a causative: he refuses to give not out of independence but because he doesn't take or doesn't wish others to take either. This tendency to read conjunctives as causatives constitutes what I later call a "strong" reading and is one of the distinctive features of wisdom interpretations.

One may properly object that all of the foregoing historical examples of quadripartite come from the same cultural milieu (Jewish, mainly first to third century) and therefore reflect formal preoccupations typical of that culture only. I should therefore like to present further historical proof-texts of particular theoretical and illustrative interest, this time Spanish Christian

2. For instance, there is the teaching that one should make one's Sabbath profane rather than depend upon others (BT Shabbat 118a; Pesahim 112a, 113a).

texts from the later Middle Ages. The first two, in addition to being presented as proverbs in their own right, continue to be paradigmatic as well in that they self-consciously illustrate a basic structure of the genre:

> All things appear good and are good, and appear bad and are bad, and appear good and are bad, and appear bad and are good. (Juan Manuel, *Lucanor* [445, lines 73–75])[3]

In paradigmatic form:

1. All things appear good and are good $(++)$
2. appear bad and are bad $(--)$
3. appear good and are bad $(+-)$
4. appear bad and are good. $(-+)$

This wisdom saying has four propositions, numbered 1 through 4. The first two propositions $(++$ and $--)$ are based on identity and are related by parallelism. They state what is or seems obvious; namely, that things are what they seem and can be (or usually are) taken at face value. The second two propositions $(+-$ and $-+)$ are based on contradiction ("and" = "but") and are related chiastically. Taken at face value, they state the two forms of that paradox especially dear to wisdom teachers, namely, that things are not what they seem. Of the two pairs, therefore, the latter seems to represent the point of the quadripartite statement. It may be the case, however, that the true point of the entire structure is the analysis of all the evaluational possibilities.

Let us take another example:

> What is dear is dear (it costs dear, it is dear to keep, it is dear to lose); what is cheap is cheap (it costs cheap, it is cheap to keep, it is cheap to lose); dear is cheap, cheap is dear. (*Lucanor* [454, lines 34–36])[4]

Structurally, the restatement is as follows:

1. dear is dear $(++)$
2. cheap is cheap $(--)$

3. "Todas las cosas paresçen bien et son buenas et paresçen mal et son malas et paresçen bien et son malas et paresçen mal et son buenas."

4. "Lo caro es caro (cuesta caro, guárdase caro, acábalo caro); Lo rehez es rehez (cuesta rehez, guárdase [G, gánase S] rehez, acábalo rehez); Lo caro es rehez, Lo rehez es caro."

3. dear is cheap $(+-)$
4. cheap is dear $(-+)$

This example repeats the basic structure and adds a partial commentary, which I have separated by parentheses rather than listed in a separate column. This is because here the commentary occurs at what may be called the first level, which is metalinguistic but not interpretive, added less to ascribe or judge value than merely to specify or control the semantic extension of the two terms being studied.

In the next example the quadripartite formula is used to structure an entire literary text:

> There are four kinds of men that one should note carefully if one wishes to live peaceful and secure lives. The first is the man who *neither says evil nor does evil* to anyone, but wishes to live in peace and loyally serve his master: he is like a good dog, who barks only when it becomes necessary to protect his master's property while defending his own person. The second kind is he who *does not speak but strikes* and naturally desires to inflict blows and does not rest unless he brings blood: he is like the dog who does not bark but bites secretly and draws blood with the intention of destroying and completely removing the one he is biting (and may God protect you from such as these . . .) The third kind of man is he who *says and does not do,* and this kind cannot do much harm, for because he says much one can guard against him, or perhaps he speaks much in order to inspire fear because he himself is afraid: and he is like the dog who barks very much but doesn't dare to bite. And the fourth kind of man is he who *says and does,* publicly and with reason and energy . . . : and he is like the good dog, which barks and bites enthusiastically when he should . . . [italics added] (*Libro del caballero Zifar* [1982, 300–301])

In this example the commentary has become so extensive as to disguise the basic quadripartite structure, which is as follows:

1. does not say and does not do (evil) $(++)$
2. does not say but does $(+-)$
3. says and does not do $(-+)$
4. says and does $(??)$[5]

5. The moral valuations in this example are rather confusing, but they seem to arise from

Of particular interest here is the expansion of the commentary at its second and more characteristic level, the presentation of illustrations taken from daily life and, with their help, the moral evaluation or interpretation of the four propositions.

The quadripartite structure was first brought into focus, as a possible descriptive model of proverbs, by G. B. Milner. Though the above full quadripartites were, unfortunately, unknown to him, Milner did cite two examples (1969c, 381) of what he called "expanded or explicit" sayings, both of which are used in French schools to teach elementary math:

Affirmer une affirmation	est une affirmation
Nier une négation	est une affirmation
Affirmer une négation	est une négation
Nier une affirmation	est une négation

A variant of this rather dry axiom takes us closer to the sages' concern for everyday life and value analysis—although, structurally speaking, the two sayings are similar:

	I	II	III
1.	The friends	of our friends	are our friends.
2.	The enemies	of our enemies	are our friends.
3.	The friends	of our enemies	are our enemies.
4.	The enemies	of our friends	are our enemies.

Lining up this saying in columns should make all the more obvious its parallel with the Abot text (5:10). Here too, column III has as its function the explicit moral commentary or evaluation of the cases presented in the four propositions.

---

statement 4, which states that the most dangerous of the four examples is one who both announces his evil intention and carries it out; this strikes one as experientially false, since the duplicity of statement 2 really poses a greater threat ("and may God protect you from such as these!"). The structural exegete therefore decided to identify statement 4 as those who speak good and do not do evil but good; statement 4 thus becomes the doublet of statement 1, where it is in fact parenthetically defined as one who does indeed bark and defend (i.e., bite) "when necessary." In terms of this interpretation, statement 4 must then be designated as $(++)$.

2. Description of Quadripartite Structures

Proceeding inductively on the basis of the foregoing examples, one can propose a description of the quadripartite logical structures of oppositions just presented, and such a formula could serve as the basis for the construction of further such structures: "A *valuational topic* or its *opposite* is *combined with* a second *valuational topic* or its *opposite* in a series of *binary propositions*, until the (*four*) logical possibilities have been exhausted." This formula is both descriptive of the full structures and prescriptive or paradigmatic. In the latter case it is this model that must be held clearly in mind for the wisdom-style analysis of actual proverbs and sayings, which more typically occur only as partial or concealed structures.

(A) VALUE (PLUS AND MINUS)

I begin with the basic assumption that proverbs are *assertions of value*. Whether this is always so is arguable, and a case can be made to except observations based on experience such as "The heart knows its own bitterness" (Prov 14:10). But until the matter is discussed more fully below and unless the contrary can be shown, I suggest that one begin with the strong assumption that a value is present; indeed, that this is the point of the proverb or saying.[6]

Based on convenience as well as on growing critical practice,[7] a positive value is indicated by a "+" and a negative value is indicated by a "−". These would typically indicate, as Milner himself put it (1969b, 55), what is "good" or "bad," useful or useless, agreeable or disagreeable, attractive or repulsive, advantageous or disadvantageous, and the like. The typically oppositional character of these valuations is discussed below.[8]

It is crucial to recall, in assigning positive and negative values to topics in sayings and proverbs, that "the point of view of the discourse and our point of view might be different" (Patte 1990b, 27), and that it is the former that is important. For example, marriage may be viewed as positive by us but as negative by a text. In such a case, marriage would be designated as a "−".

---

6. See Chapter 3.2, "The Argument of Value."

7. Cf. Milner (1969a–c), Dundes (1981), Fontaine (1982), and Van Leeuwen (1988).

8. I am thus in full agreement with Grzybek (1987, 57) when he states that " 'good' and 'bad' is the most essential feature expressed in paremiology," but I would specify that although any given evaluations must be derived from the ideology of the text in question, these can be further generated or extended by purely structural means, notably oppositions.

This helps avoid arbitrariness in assigning values and insures that proverb analysis will remain focused on the text and its own value system.

(B) RELATIVE VALUES

Wisdom sayings are statements of relative value or *valuational propositions*. In my theoretical restatements of wisdom sayings, the listing of propositions from 1 through 4 indicates an order of axiological distinction and (usually) priority. This priority of values can be configured vertically, according to one of two possible paradigms:

1. good	1. the best
2. not bad[9]	2. better than 3
3. not good	3. worse than 2
4. bad	4. the worst

The explicit dominance of relative valuation in the full structures, as reflected in such forms as better-than proverbs, seems to suggest that the main purpose of such statements and structures is to assign relative value, whether explicitly or implicitly.

(C) VALUATIONAL TOPICS

Not infrequently, critics have yielded to grammatical and syntactical denominations such as "subject" and "predicate" to indicate the basic units of proverbs. These can indeed be convenient, since it is often the case that the grammatical subject corresponds with the first member of a proposition and the grammatical predicate with the second. But many propositions are composed of two grammatical subjects and many more of two predicates ("gives and takes," "says and does"); such an approach is too bound to particular languages and thus impedes an intercultural study of proverbs.

There is another critical practice, originating in linguistics and applied to paremiology by Fontaine (1982, 34–38) and Van Leeuwen (1988, 47–50), of describing the (two) basic elements of each proverb as "Topic plus Comment." A case has been made (Dundes 1981, 57–60) for defining the minimum structure of proverbs as consisting of one descriptive element (topic +

---

9. See Chapter 3.2.c.

comment), and this approach has the merit of describing the actual or explicit form of proverbs in whatever language. But this advantage is also a liability, since actual form can in fact conceal meaning and structure. For Dundes, thus, Saint Paul's "it is better to marry than to burn" would be a "minimum descriptive element." I shall later argue, however, that structurally speaking this is misleading and that this statement actually implies two fuller propositions: "marry and not burn" and "not marry and burn," and conceals two others: "marry and burn" and "not marry and not burn." Second, there is a hidden logical connective here (as well as a hidden term) expressing a condition. Thus, "it is better to marry *only if* it leads to not burning." Third, it should be noted that valuations (positive or negative) are not necessarily apparent from the saying itself. For example, in "it is better to marry than to burn" or "it is better to give than to receive," it is not at all clear that in the first the two topics are negative and in the second they are positive. But it is clear that such "minimum descriptive elements" are better thought of as (e)valuational than descriptive.

(D) **W**ISDOM VALUES AND **w**ORLDLY VALUES

What is more interesting in wisdom sayings is that one topic often refers to physical or worldly reality (what can be termed the **w** value or topic), whereas the second of two topics is more often related to **W**isdom values (here termed **W**). Thus, "Better a dry morsel with peace[10] (**W**) than a house full of feasting (**w**) with strife" (Prov 17:1). **W** values are basic, central values of wisdom, whereas the **w** terms are tentative, potentially conflictive with **W** but, structurally speaking, more properly conceived as contextual, as test-cases for **W** values. Since they also receive "+" and "−" valuations, however, **W** values are potential contradictions of **w** values, or perhaps, to use a Stoic term, indifferent to them, and vice versa. In this example, the worldly possibility of a sumptuous banquet tests the wisdom value of peace. In the Juan Manuel example of "appear good and are bad," the **w** value of appearances is played against the **W** value of truth (cf. Finkielkraut's distinction between factual value and truth, Chapter 4, n. 22). In the Hilkiah tale, the **w** value of *politesse* has no standing, despite the astonishment of even the two rabbis, when confronted with the **W** value of honesty.

---

10. RSV: "quiet," for the Hebrew *shalwah*, which, however, is equated with peace (*shalom*) in Ps 122:7.

(E) BINARY PROPOSITIONS

Binary propositions do not always occur in nature, so to speak, and often must be teased out from the givens, the valuational topics and their opposites. As Roger D. Abrahams (1972, 21) nicely put it, "not all proverbs fully state their descriptive proposition; one element may simply be implied." Thus, rather than being actual statements of a proverb as it occurs in performance, a proposition may elliptically state only one of the four logical binary (**W** + **w**) possibilities implicit in the terms or valuational topics, and it is only in the fully elaborated quadripartite that all four propositions are explicit.[11] Thus, to review the example cited above, Saint Paul's formal better-than statement is to be interpreted as an assertion of the relative superiority of one proposition over a second one: to marry and not burn/not to marry and burn; Paul's single statement thus implies *two* propositions, each only partially stated, and further implies two others, as we shall see in the next section.

It is clear, therefore, that each proposition is binary, and such a binary proposition can be termed a "minimum logical element." For my purposes this term is preferable to Dundes's "minimum descriptive element" in that I am describing not actual forms but rather implicit or deep structural units. Thus, to repeat, each proposition is *binary*, made up of *two different* valuational topics, no more and no less. Each topic (or its opposite) appears in each proposition throughout the structure, generating three further propositions consistent with the logical possibilities of such structures.

(F) OPPOSITIONS

Valuational topics have two levels of meaning: on a semantic level they derive their positive (or negative) meaning from wisdom or cultural values; on a logical level they derive their meaning *relationally, each with its own opposite.*[12]

The concept of *opposite* is usually that of simple negation. Thus, the opposite of "say" is "not say," and the opposite of "not say" is "say." Any term of

11. I am drawn to L. Waugh's distinction: "*Elliptical structures* are those in which certain signs have been left out, but are assumed to be known to the addressee, while *explicit structures* are those fully replete with signs" (cited in Berlin 1985, 16).

12. Saussure regards values in linguistics as based on oppositions: "Instead of pre-existing ideas then, we find . . . values emanating from the [linguistic] system. When they are said to correspond to concepts, it is understood that the concepts are purely differential and defined not by their positive content but negatively by their relations with the other terms of the system. Their most precise characteristic is in being what the others are not" (1959, 117).

content (valuational topic) may thus serve as a starting point in the genera-tion of meaning, and the first logical step would be to notice its simple opposite.

To be distinguished from simple negation is the concept of contradiction or dialectical opposition. Jameson (1972, 164) has offered the following explanation: "Our starting point (the choice of the content of S) is in reality a binary opposition, for it is bound to include within itself a concept of its own anti-S, its own dialectical opposite." It thus serves to "enjoin upon us the obligation to articulate any apparent free-standing concept or term into that binary opposition which it structurally presupposes and which forms the very basis of its intelligibility." For example, the simple opposite of "good" would be "not good" whereas the contradiction would be "bad."[13] Logically, the difference between the two is significant; in the practice of wisdom writing, however, this difference is of no consequence in the percep-tion of opposite values at the level of individual topics, so that "generous," for example, could generate as its opposite valuational topic either "ungenerous" or "downright stingy." It should be carefully noted, however, that this is not the case in evaluative comparisons *between* propositions, since "not bad" is distinct from and superior to both "bad" and "not good."[14]

Since valuational topics are by definition *oppositional* (**W** and not-**W**, **w** and not-**w**), they may be represented by (+) and (−), used here as signs of *structural* opposition—which of course correspond to positive and negative values within the wisdom or within the culture being described. This exploits Milner's brilliant suggestion (1969a–c) but avoids his problem of trying to apply subjective values (i.e., those of the interpreter or critic, or those which the latter thinks appropriate) to the various segments of propositions, since positive and negative are, at this level, not only semantic but relational. Plus and minus are thus considered elements of structure as well as of meaning, and "structure is more or less independent of meaning although to be sure there will always be conscious or unconscious meanings attached to any given [elements in the] structure" (Dundes 1981, 56). This convention of plus and minus has the further advantage, once the valuations become established through intratextual or extratextual commentary, of facilitating the moral interpretation of the total statement or structure. However, such knowledge

13. Or, to take an example from anthropology: beginning with the term "marriage," the simple negation would be "adultery" (relationships that are not matrimonial) whereas the contradiction would be "incest," indicating relationships that are proscribed (Jameson 1972, 163). This contradictory kind of negation can be found in wisdom texts, but it is far less frequent than that of simple opposition.

14. See Chapter 3.2.c, "Relative Value."

is not necessary to the study of proverb structure, which depends, at this level, on the simple, logical opposition between the two poles of any topic.[15]

An interesting corollary is that the "+" and "−" values may or may not accompany their assigned members for the duration of the structure; thus, "cheap" may have a negative moral value in one proposition and a positive one in another. For example, observe in Milner's example, already cited above, the shifting value of the first or "I" term:

	I	II	III
1.	The friends	of our friends	are our friends.
2.	The enemies	of our enemies	are our friends.
3.	The friends	of our enemies	are our enemies.
4.	The enemies	of our friends	are our enemies.

Note that in column II, which seems to express the major value of this saying (one's own friends or enemies), valuations are assigned per se or a priori: "friends" are "+" and "enemies" are "−". In column I, however, value is assigned relationally, with the result that "enemies," while remaining "−" in proposition 4, receives a "+" value in proposition 2. This occasions no structural crisis, however, since the other term of the binary in column I will also shift its valuation and the quadripartite structure will remain stable or in equilibrium: "friends" remains positive in proposition 1 but becomes negative in 3. The basic quadripartite structure is thus a *stable* structure in that its pluses and minuses are always in equilibrium.[16]

15. Parenthetically, my difference with Milner, other than the manner of assigning positive and negative values, is that he considers "(+ −) and (− +)" to be a full quadripartite structure, whereas I consider it to be only a half of such a structure. Milner thus speaks of parts or segments or quadrants, whereas I speak of minimum units (that is to say, two valuational topics). From Milner's point of view two criticisms may be leveled against me. The first is that his examples, though consisting of only two propositions, are yet full structures. My answer is that his examples (1969a, 55–57) fall largely into two categories: (a) observations, which escape both structures since they are not constructed on binaries; (b) structures of cause and result, to which the quadripartite structure, according to my own definition, is admittedly recalcitrant (although, I quickly add, perceived in the interpretive act). A second criticism would be that he is speaking of proverbs and I am not, meaning that all his examples are concrete metaphors taken from experience. This is true, but at the level of analysis, proverbs must be reduced to abstract "sayings" in order to be interpreted, and at this level my examples are sayings no less than his. For example, "there is no smoke without fire" must first be generalized into something like "signs are revealing" before being applied once again to one's particular situation. For good criticisms of Milner, see Grzybek (1987, 55–58), and C. T. Scott (1976); also see Chapter 4.3.

16. In this saying column III, structurally speaking, expresses the commentary or evaluation of each proposition, which I typically designate by combinations of pluses and minuses. Thus:

(G) LOGICAL CONNECTIVES

In each of the four propositions, the valuational topics are combined by various *logical connectives* throughout the structure. In particular, the following are illustrated here:

1. equivalence: "cheap *is* (or *is not*) cheap." In such sample texts there is a perfect balance between the two: two *equational* statements or propositions based on the (false) identity of topics, and two *contrastive* propositions based on the difference of topics. That is to say, all four propositions are cast in equational frames (A "is" B, or A "is not" B).

2. causation: This is also known as implication (A "leads to" B) and, following G. von Rad (1972) and others, the "act/consequence relationship."

3. conjunction: In samples such as "giving and taking" there is a series of propositions that are complementary, meaning that their forms are *conjunctive* (A "and" B).

4. possession: "the tail *of* a lion," a "friend *of* a friend."

It should be carefully noted that the explicit form of the connective is not necessarily expressive of the logical value being asserted. This is particularly true of the conjunctive "and," especially in Hebrew texts, since the *waw*-connective, in addition to "and," can also be read as "but, for the purpose of, since, although," and the like. Indeed, the discussion of the particular kind of logical relatedness is one of the key points of focus in interpretation.

———————

$$1.\ (++)$$
$$2.\ (+-)$$
$$3.\ (--)$$
$$4.\ (-+)$$

Van Leeuwen (1988) would call columns I and II the relational topics (RT) and column III the comment (C). Thus, according to him and perfectly in keeping with Milner's example, column III can be adequately described as follows:

$$1.\ \ldots +$$
$$2.\ \ldots +$$
$$3.\ \ldots -$$
$$4.\ \ldots -$$

However, it is always important to refer back to the relational topics in order to reflect further on the finer distinctions between the two pluses 1 and 2 and the two minuses 3 and 4. In this text, for example, there are important distinctions implied in "better the enemy of a friend" (4) as opposed to "the friend of an enemy" (3).

Typically and as noted in the case of the complete quadripartites, once a particular connective is chosen, it persists throughout that structure. Relations of comparison (e.g., better-than) do not operate within propositions but rather between them, as stated above.[17]

(H) SEMANTIC RELEVANCE AND RELATEDNESS

From the above it is clear that a statement such as "John is tall" will not meet the minimum qualifications of a quadripartite (or, for that matter, of a wisdom saying), nor does such a claim as "what is mine is good and what is yours is bad." For, although each has a topic placed on a valuational grid, it has no second valuational topic and is thus a mere assertion of value and not a *comparative* evaluation. By this I do not deny that John may be being valued as "tall" or that "mine" is being favorably compared to "yours," but there is no evaluation (what I call *contextualization*) in terms of a second value. Even "haste makes waste" can be evaluated from a wisdom perspective only if delivered in response to a view such as "haste makes profit" and, moreover, is perhaps considered wise only if the oppositional advice "deliberation makes profit" is perceived. It may in fact be the case, as Van Leeuwen has indicated in a private communication, that such a proverb in fact "presupposes such a logico-linguistic structure [as the quadripartite] in order to signify," even that "such paradigmatic awareness of options is required for understanding" any such utterance. My point, as I shall go on to argue, is that the sages made explicit these implicit structures and further emphasized their importance for proverb analysis.

There are surely requirements of *relevance* as well. Topics have to be of interest to the group; they have to express values important to the speaker. Thus, "Chung is wise and Ching is stupid" would be disqualified to a Spanish audience; similarly, the observation "mountains are high and valleys are low" would seem to qualify only if applied metaphorically, as in Isa 40:4.

The issues of semantic relevance and relatedness often occur together. In the context of Jewish values, for example, one finds many expressions of the view that "it is better to be poor than quarrel." But one would be hard put to find a saying such as "it is better to remain celibate than quarrel," since

---

17. In his otherwise excellent article, Abrahams (1972, 120) limits the discussion of logical connectives to causation and equivalence.

celibacy is not regarded as a positive value. In other words, topics must be real options in terms of the given culture.

Finally, recall that the basic structure may or may not be accompanied by a *commentary*. In our sample texts two levels were distinguished. Interpretative commentary is always invoked at the level of the application of cultural values, at the point at which the text attempts to identify the carriers of the values being proposed. Thus, one who "gives and doesn't take" is identified in a commentary as "a saintly man." This commentary is outside the quadripartite framework proper, but its elaboration is facilitated, even encouraged and required, by the structure.

(I) FOUR

The basic architectural *structure* is composed of *four* statements or propositions, and this is the basis for calling it quadripartite. Despite the form or style of presentation of a proverb or saying, a complete quadripartite may be implied and in fact is tacitly assumed when a wisdom proverb is interpreted, as we shall see. For example, the partial structure "says and does" implies three further propositions, generated through logical relationships implicit in the deep structure. The structure of particular interest to the present study seems based on the fact that *four* is a pervasive and stable deep-structure, what Lévi-Strauss called a model. Whether this particular structure is to be related to the Jungian mandala, as G. B. Milner (1969a, 70) speculated, is far from an idle matter but is one that goes beyond structural studies.

More pertinent to recent structural studies of the Bible is that our quadripartite shares many characteristics with Greimas's semiotic square, which he refers to as an "elementary structure of signification" (cf. Frederic Jameson on Greimas 1987, xvi). To give but a single example, taken from what is proving to be a most fruitful application of this structure to biblical studies, consider Daniel Patte's elaboration of Heschel's metaphor "Sabbath is a palace (in time)." Patte (1990a, 149–51) begins by noticing the opposites of the two terms; thus,

$$\begin{aligned} \text{Sabbath} &<> \text{weekday} \\ \text{Palace} &<> \text{slums.} \end{aligned}$$

He then goes on to state the full structure as follows:

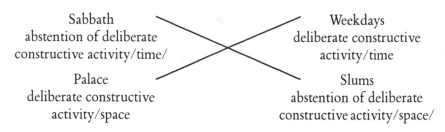

Sabbath — Weekdays
abstention of deliberate — deliberate constructive
constructive activity/time/ — activity/time

Palace — Slums
deliberate constructive — abstention of deliberate
activity/space — constructive activity/space/

In terms of my quadripartite above, this diagram would allow the following four possibilities:

Sabbath + palace $(++)$
weekday + slums $(--)$
Sabbath + slums $(+-)$
weekday + palace $(-+)$

In spite of the remarkable similarity of these two models, two differences can be noticed at this point. The first is that Patte's model, based on Greimasian linguistics, is a paradigm in Lévi-Strauss's sense of being a pure theoretical construct that can be derived logically,[18] whereas the quadripartite studied here is a constructive and interpretative structure in actual use by its practitioners, thus having an historical as well as a theoretical basis (less sophisticated, to be sure!). The second difference concerns use. The older model, for example, would allow the generation of such evaluative sayings as the following: "Better the Sabbath, even in the slums, than a palace." Or, "better the slums on the Sabbath than a weekday even in a palace." Patte's analysis, by contrast, is intent on specifying the ways in which the original metaphor is to be interpreted. Here, for instance, Patte's caption to the diagram postulates that the figure "Sabbath is a Palace" has relevance to "Building Process." It is fair to say, however, that Patte's kind of analysis would be required before the second kind of (moral) evaluation can take place.

18. Todorov (1970, chap. 1) has offered a theoretical discussion of this point as applied to genre, namely that "the science of logic precedes the science of nature" (cf. *MF:* 20, no. 63).

2

FORMS OF WISDOM
Expressions and Transformations of Quadripartite Structures

1. Full and Concealed Structure

The pedagogic and analytic functions of the remarkable quadripartite examples considered in Chapter 1 seem obvious. Their authors are intent on teaching important values, and the teaching is performed by an intellectual analysis that carefully enumerates all logical possibilities and distinguishes their types. Perhaps less apparent, but equally noteworthy, is their value as models of how real proverbs are constructed and how they work. It is especially this third function that interests me at this point: how the quadripartite model can provide insight into the form and, progressively, the meaning of proverbs and proverb thinking.

On the basis of a description of these remarkable historical samples, which constitute full or complete ("expanded or explicit") quadripartite structures in their own right, it would be possible to offer an adequate generative model for proverbs.[1] This would be some-

---

1. Proceeding on the basis of Greimas's assumption (1970, 309) that "la description schématique et structurale du plan du signifiant rendra compte des configurations de leur [proverbes et dictons] signifié."

what misleading, however, since quadripartites typically do not occur in such full form but rather concealed, and structural analysis is necessary to make this meaning explicit (reasons for this subterfuge will be discussed later). Take, for example, the following saying:

Ce sont les petites pluies qui gâtent les grands chemins.

It is small rains that ruin great highways.

The actual form of this proverb is paradoxical and misleading: why would small rains have more destructive power than larger ones?[2] The meaning becomes clear only when one perceives a second and implicit sense of "small," that is, "small but frequent." Thus, paradigmatically, "small but frequent" is better than "large but infrequent"; or, to use a popular variant: "Slowly but surely the bird builds its nest" ("Petit à petit l'oiseau fait son nid"). Also, the qualifier "great" has no relation to the meaning and is added merely to enhance the moral of assiduousness: frequency can achieve even big results. Thus, the implicit structure is the following:

1. large and frequent $(++)$
2. small and frequent $(-+)$
3. large and infrequent $(+-)$
4. small and infrequent $(--)$

To offer a more typical example, consider Saint Paul's well-known dictum, already mentioned above: "It is better to marry than to burn (RSV: be aflame with passion)" (1 Corinthians 7:9). The absurdity or perhaps limitation of the literal message was well understood by Rabelais's incontinent Panurge, who sensed that he would be aflame even if he were to marry.[3] For the saying to

---

2. Or, to point out another problem: do such rains ruin only large highways but not small ones? (This second problem is of lesser weight, for one understands, a fortiori, that if it ruins large ones it surely ruins them all.) Take a further example:

Bien dire fait rire,
Bien faire fait taire.

One does not stop to wonder at the truth value of the first part of this proverb (why indeed should fine speaking produce ridicule?), which obviously can stand only if the implicit "sans bien faire," "without good deeds," is also grasped at some level. I view such proverbs as deliberately concealing part of the truth (and structure) in order to produce effects such as humor (cf. Chapter 3.1.d.), and perhaps also to provoke annoyance and analysis.

3. See Rabelais's *Tiers livre.* Panurge would continue to burn either because his lust is insatiable or,

carry Paul's meaning, therefore, the implicit assertions must be spelled out. This text actually asserts two propositions: That to marry and not burn is "better than" not to marry and burn. But this does not exhaust the logical possibilities of the two topics of this text (marrying and burning), which can generate two further propositions by the simple recombination of the opposites of the two terms. Thus, in the order of best to worst, the following quadripartite structure arises:

1. not marry and not burn $(++)$
2. marry and not burn $(-+)$
3. not marry and burn $(+-)$
4. marry and burn $(--)$

Through the implicit presence of the two extremes, which are either "better than" proposition 2 and "worse than" proposition 3, we are able to deduce the author's entire value system with respect to the topics under discussion. Subsequent commentary could easily supply illustrations. Of the two implied propositions 1 and 4, the first could refer to the Perfect (later the contemplatives), while the fourth could aptly describe cuckolded spouses. The difference in focus seems to be based on whether the wisdom writer is addressing those for whom only the best matters, or whether he has in mind intermediate levels of wisdom such as that pursued by warriors and family people. Better-than statements address the latter, and in this text Saint Paul is referring to either failed contemplatives or the married who manage to achieve both good sexual relations and also enough sanctification to avoid cuckoldry and infidelity.

Parenthetically, it may be observed that in this example the positive or "+" and negative or "−" values have been assigned according to Paul's own value system. Different values would involve a redistribution, although the general characteristics of the whole (i.e., the stability or balance between positive and negative values) would remain similar. Tristan and Iseult, for instance, who are against marriage but in favor of the excitement of desire, might generate the following:

1. not marry and burn (with desire) $(++)$
2. marry and burn (e.g., the lovers in the forest living like man
   and wife and separated by the naked sword) $(-+)$

---

with greater probability, because he would get the wife he deserves; that is, one unfaithful like himself, and he would thus burn with jealousy rather than unsatisfied lust.

3. not marry and not burn $(+-)$
4. marry and not burn $(--)$

This structure would generate the following better-than dictum: "It is better to marry (if that would stimulate desire) than not burn," a point of view not inconsistent with the doctrine of courtly love. Here "marry" would be the contextual or **w** value and "not burning" would be the major or **W**isdom value. In this context, of course, no connection with the wisdom tradition is implied, although the ideology of courtly love certainly had its own normative or absolute values.

As interesting as the interpretation of such sayings may be, my purpose at this point is to consider not their content but rather the structure through which their message is presented. Of particular interest is the existence of four evaluative possibilities for each text. In the first examples such as the BT Qiddushin text ("righteous and good") the statements are explicit; they in fact constitute the form of analysis. In the Saint Paul text, the four statements are implicit (two in part and the other two completely) and must be teased out through analysis. However, the presence of a similar paradigm in both texts recapitulates our two methods of proceeding: historical or descriptive, and theoretical or analytical. Although the second would be sufficient for the purposes of developing a theoretical model, the fact that the wisdom tradition has preserved an impressive number of pure or full structures is of great interest. The quadripartite is thus not only a modern construct but also a paradigmatic model based on actual historical use, and this remarkable situation, as previously stated, imposes the obligation to refer modern theory and research to earlier attempts by the wisdom writers themselves.

I wish to distinguish my present interest in form from what is known as the "form-critical interpretation" that has been practiced for decades in biblical criticism and that is currently having a fair hearing in such publications as the series "The Forms of Old Testament Literature." That enterprise addresses much broader questions than the present inquiry and in greater number. Specifically, according to that methodology there are four orders of analysis: a text's structure (which includes the total literary structure of a work and its thematics), its genre, setting (usually social), and intention.[4] By contrast, my initial focus is much narrower and more akin to "rhetorical criticism." It hovers close to literary style and its repetitive formulas and techniques, and especially those smaller units such as the

4. See especially Murphy (1981) and the statement of the general aims of the series (ix–xi).

"propositions" analyzed above that are expressive of value through deep structure.

2. Equational Proverbs ($+$ is $+$), ($-$ is $-$)

Our daily speech abounds with equational proverbs. Who has not heard such expressions as "cheap is cheap," "boys will be boys," "a bargain is a bargain," "business is business," "enough is enough." Although such equational proverbs constitute a basic ingredient of our proverb repertoire, it is no less true that folklorists rarely mention them in their collections (Golopentia-Eretescu 1965, 1972), perhaps because they seem to say nothing. A notable exception is Juan Manuel, who lists so many instances of this type that one suspects a fascination, to say the least, and perhaps even an unusual case of identity crisis. A closer look at these remarkable texts may suggest some of the "wisdom" uses of such proverbs. Consider the following texts:

> If love is good love it is love.[5]
>
> Good life is life.[6]
>
> A king [who is a] king ... [7]
>
> If a man is a man ... [8]
>
> A deed is a deed when a deed does the deed.[9]
>
> An error is an error.[10]

Note that these analytical statements do not always occur in their pristine state; they often include a commentary that orients the interpretation. In *Lucanor* this marker is often "good," explicitly stated in the first two samples and implied in the next three. Further, the conditions of identity are also

5. "Si amor es buen amor, es amor" *Lucanor* 459, line 143.
6. "Vida buena, vida es" *Lucanor* 459, line 148.
7. "El rey rey ... " *Lucanor* 448, line 151.
8. "Si el omne es omne" *Lucanor* 457, line 91.
9. "El fecho es fecho quando el fecho faze el fecho" *Lucanor* 450, lines 187–88. In opposition to Barry Paul Taylor (1983, 272f.), I take this saying to be a clarification of the basic term *fecho*. Thus, "a deed is a real deed when the deed itself (and not *ventura*, 'chance') performs (causes or motivates) the deed."
10. "El yerro es yerro" *Lucanor* 458, line 123.

specified: "an X is a good or real X when or only if..." Thus, the equational proposition "a man(a) is a man(b)" allows Juan Manuel to distinguish (a) the label indicating actual or usual usage, man as a psycho-socio-physical being (a **w**-value) from (b) the morally "good" man (a Wisdom or **W**-value).[11] In this way wisdom registers its objection to current or popular usage and insists that the label should more properly be applied to moral and spiritual values. This insistence that designations such as "king," "love," or "man" be taken primarily in their moral (rather than their usual or physical or literal) sense is a major tactic of wisdom writers. It may be viewed as an attempt to "purify the dialect of the tribe" (T. S. Eliot, based on Mallarmé) or to emphasize that its own sense of important value-words is the primary one. Consider the one-upmanship recounted in the following anecdote:

> A prince once said to Socrates: "I am worried about you." He asked him why. The prince replied: "Because I see your poverty and need." He said to him: "If you really knew what poverty is, you would worry about your soul's poverty and pay no attention to my poverty." (*MF*:21, lines 2–5)

The upshot is that all such terms come to be perceived as oppositional, depending on whether the usual or the wisdom meaning is stressed. Thus, in such anecdotes the usual sense of "poverty" as "lack of money" is provocatively attributed by wisdom writers to one who is "rich" in knowledge or deeds, so that calling him "poor" seems imprecise, even outrageous. Hence the Rabbinic saying, intended to be paradoxical: "There is no poverty except poverty of knowledge" (BT Nedarim 41a). Similarly, Shakespeare uses a wisdom tactic in playing off wealth against "*love's* wealth" ("Taming of the Shrew").

Of course, just as pure identities (or pure oppositions) do not exist in experience, they do not occur in such proverbs either (Crépeau 1975, 294–95); in the same way, pure repetition is also impossible (Barthes 1972, 79). This can be grasped more clearly at the structural level if each "equational" proposition is seen to be composed of values functioning at two different levels, typically the intersection of **w**-values, referring to worldly or common experience, with **W**-values. Thus, "the good is good" can typically be read as "a good action is to be judged as morally good." Of course, the

---

11. Note that three further meanings are excluded in Juan Manuel's "wisdom" application: (a) "and not more" (as in Montaigne's quip that even a king still sits upon his arse and is therefore "not more than" a man); (b) "and not less"; (c) "not more or less."

functions can be reversed. In English, for example, a different intonation such as "the *good* is good" could mean "only what is morally good can be considered praiseworthy or effective."

It is true that if the interpretation of such proverbs is restricted to the literal level and receives what can be called a weak reading, then their interpretative range is reduced considerably. Let us again consider one of the *Lucanor* sample texts as an example of the interpretative value of the second topic in each proposition:

1. dear is dear
2. cheap is cheap
3. dear is cheap
4. cheap is dear

Propositions 1 and 2 are near tautologies only if both terms are taken literally: you have to pay a lot for goods that are worth a lot, whereas valueless things can be purchased for little. Even here we are not really dealing with tautologies but rather assertions or observations of the general equivalence between cost and monetary value. However, if "dear is dear" is taken as wisely judgmental (what is expensive is valuable because *it will end up*[12] being less expensive or cheaper), then this is already a statement of proposition 3. Thus, if the choice is made from the start to read the first two (equational) propositions metaphorically or "wisely," then the second pair of propositions, the oppositionals, becomes the correct commentary or translation or wisdom restatement of the first pair. It should be noted that this "wise" reading does not jump registers in its evaluation, so to speak, but rather remains within the monetary realm.

Let us try to state this important point in different terms. If one were to imagine an axis with identificational features at one end and contrastive features at the other, then, it is claimed, equational proverbs would fall close to the identificational end (Dundes 1981, 53). It seems to me, however, that if such statements are indeed completely identificational (i.e., if the two valuational topics of the statement are perfectly synonymous), then they are of no interest, since no one goes around observing that "blue is blue" or "the sky is the sky." Even in the equationals just examined, the equation asserts contrasts rather than identifications: "What people often call 'man' is the opposite of a true man." I would therefore like to propose that equational proverbs of the

12. Observations are, of course, also judgmental, but by "*wisely* judgmental" the sages referred to what the results would be *in the long run* (see Chapter 4.4).

type "cheap is cheap" and "enough is enough" are only formal identities, since what is being asserted (by wisdom teachers) is the oppositional form: "cheap is really expensive," and "enough is really too much."[13] In other words, and this is my main point, identificational binaries are oppositional binaries in disguise, and in a typical wisdom reading the redundancies ($+$ is $+$) and ($-$ is $-$) really mean the oppositions ($+$ is $-$), ($-$ is $+$).

This development within identificational propositions, wherein equationals become transmuted into oppositionals because of the ambivalence of the topic, recurs between pairs of such propositions as well. Just as one of the identical propositions logically generates the other ("bad is bad" generates "good is good"), analogously one of the oppositional propositions logically generates its opposite. Thus, if "good is bad," then it is implied that "bad is good." These pairs now challenge one another, since each claims to exhaust all of reality and thus denies the other. In other words, each oppositional proposition does two things: it implies its complement and also denies both equational propositions (which are thus obviously inferred from the structure, if only to be denied).[14] Thus, the equational statements are in complementary distribution one with the other. Each structure is composed of a pair of equational propositions and a pair of oppositional propositions; since each pair is in complementary distribution, the two pairs cannot logically reside within the same structure unless adjustments are made at the level of interpretation.[15]

3. Better-Than Proverbs

Stylistically speaking, there exists a most important category of sayings that is easily recognizable through its formulaic "better-than" component. These sayings are frequent in traditional wisdom literature, beginning even before the Book of Proverbs, which has numerous explicit instances. However, all proverbs are better-than insofar as they imply evaluation and comparison of

13. Or, in the biblical formula *rab lakem,* "you have gone *too* far"; literally, "this is (too) much to you" (Num. 16:3).

14. Observe that the term "oppositional" is here extended beyond the generation of "opposites" (see Chapter 1.2.f) at the level of topic. Thus, in equational sayings two levels of opposition occur: (a) each statement is formed from a contrasting semantic pair; here it is the topics that are oppositional; (b) the oppositional statement is in opposition to the equational pairs but not to the other oppositional statement, with which it is in complementary distribution.

15. These wisdom adjustments are further studied below in Chapter 3.1.e, "What's What."

values, and the actual forms of the comparison can offer numerous variations. One possibility is the *injunction,* such as "*be* a tail to lions and *be not* a head to foxes" (Abot 4:15), which nevertheless implies a comparison and can thus be easily restated as the two intermediate members of the usual quadripartite structure, as seen above. Another instance, where mere juxtaposition implies a comparison, is the following: "The fool is small even if he is old; the sage is great even if he is a lad" (*MF:*41, no. 26). Here the characterizations "small" and "great" serve as commentary and imply a comparison. Thus, we see the format of the already established propositions 2 and 3:

> 2. lad and sage $(-+)$
> 3. old and fool $(+-)$

Also, one must list as formal variants of better-than all formulas that state "*x* than," such as *easier than:* "It is easier to remove a happy man from his happiness than a sad man from his sadness" (*MF:*19, no. 40). This is actually a better-than structure in which the third member is stated before the second. Thus:

> 3. happy man and removed happiness $(+-)$
> 2. sad man and removed sadness $(-+)$[16]

In terms of structure, better-than proverbs occupy the intermediate positions 2 and 3 in the chain of four, meaning that they typically have the values of $(-+)$ and $(+-)$, in contrast with the implied "best" and "worst." That is to say, there is always one possibility better-than the better of the two and always one possibility worse-than the worse of the two. "Better than" thus means better than proposition 3 and certainly better than proposition 4 but not the best of all possibilities.

If, as I proposed above, each of the four propositions of a quadripartite may be described as a topic plus a predicate or second valuational topic, then in many wisdom contexts the latter is of such a nature as to render palatable or "better" a value that would normally be considered worse or even unthinkable. For example, from the text of Abot (4:15) cited above, the following quadripartite is implied:

> 1. head of lions $(++)$
> 2. tail of lions $(-+)$

16. This saying is further discussed in Chapter 3.2.c, "Relative Value."

3. head of foxes $(+-)$
4. tail of foxes $(--)$

The better-than proverb, comprised of propositions 2 and 3, thus presents the exception that proves the rule, according to which it is understood that heads are better than tails, except under the specified condition.[17]

It thus seems possible to discover a given culture's major (**Wisdom**) values by simply reviewing the predicates or wisdom topics of proposition 2 in a list of such structures. For the Book of Proverbs, the following occur: work, fear of God, love, righteousness, lowliness of spirit, slowness to anger, quiet (peace), integrity, openness, nearness, and wisdom.[18] It seems to me that further theoretical development of such listings could benefit greatly from Max Kadushin's method of value analysis, as focused by his term "value concept."[19]

To consider the matter from a slightly different perspective, in such structures what is typically compared in the intermediate propositions are the two negatives. Thus, Saint Paul's formulation actually highlights the key terms in such a way as to suggest that the force of the comparison is not "better than" but "worse than": "what is worse than marrying: burning." Examples abound: "Better a man despised who has a job than one who plays the great man but lacks bread" (Prov 12:9). Thus:

2. lowly but eats $(-+)$
3. takes pride (by not working) and goes hungry $(+-)$

Here also, the force of the contrast resides between the two negatives, the negative of proposition 2 being better than the negative of proposition 3. Again: "It is better to live in a corner of the roof than in a spacious house with a contentious woman" (Prov 21:9; see also 21:19). Rabbi Nachmiash remarks that "although both are bad, the one is better than the other, as in Lam 4:9: 'Better those killed by the sword than by hunger'" (Keil 1983, 150). A related example: "It is better for us to serve the Egyptians than to die in the wilderness" (Exod 14:12).

Or, again: "It is better to eat brown bread than to depend on another." That is to say:

17. For a different statement of this phenomenon, see Chapter 3.2.e, "Beyond Compare."
18. Cf. Bryce (1972b, 350); Murphy (1981, 67); Crenshaw, however (in a private communication), finds the four cardinal virtues of Egyptian wisdom more appropriate to biblical wisdom: timeliness, integrity, restraint, and eloquence.
19. For an excellent presentation and analysis, see the collection of essays by Ochs (1990).

2. brown bread but one's own $(-+)$
3. white bread but another's $(+-)$

In addition to being comparisons or, rather, contrasts, such texts also suggest a kind of puzzle or riddle in which one is challenged to imagine the absurd: "When is it better to be a tail than a head?" Or "when is hatred better than love?" When, in other words, is it possible that the negative of proposition 2 can be better than the negative or even the positive of proposition 3? Such a perspective provides a paradigm for considering all forms of negativity (pain, death, absence), which become superior to their opposites (but not the best of all possible situations) through their origin from or alliance with God or **W**isdom or some other major positive value.

If within each proposition of the better-than structures examined above the valuation often follows the last member, this may be because in our languages it is the second member that usually carries the stronger evaluation and it is the first that is the contextual topic proper. Thus, $(-+)$ would be "better than" $(+-)$. But two other reasons suggest themselves: (a) the presence of one (not two) major values such as **W**-values (e.g., wisdom, God, peace); (b) the nature of the logical connective between the two terms of a proposition. In this latter respect there appears to be a major difference between the possessives studied above (e.g., "the tail *of* a lion") and another major class, the conjunctives /disjunctives: $(+ \ and \ +)$, $(- \ and \ +)$ $(+ \ and \ -)$ $(- \ and \ -)$. In wisdom texts this is a most frequent pattern. Recall the following sample text (Abot 5:10):

1. doesn't give and doesn't take $(-+)$
2. gives and takes $(+-)$
3. gives and doesn't take $(++)$
4. doesn't give and takes $(--)$

Here the two topics (giving and taking) are complementary and, taken together, form a complete category. But neither is a dominant value to the exclusion of the other, and one would be hard put to discover which of the traditional better-than propositions is preferred by the author of this passage. Would the following be the correct order, or would the reverse be preferred:

1. doesn't give and doesn't take $(-+)$
2. gives and takes $(+-)$

The reason may be that, whereas possession (by a **W**-value) virtually transforms the value of a **w**-topic into its opposite, as seen above, conjunction is a weaker and more equal relation between terms. Thus, the valuation of the mixed binary propositions $(+-)$ and $(-+)$ takes on special importance in conjunctive structures, given that both are not only mixed but also theoretically equal. This is the issue of semantic relatedness described above.[20]

4. Proverbs of Simple Preference

The first part of this study assumes that the quadripartite structure is theoretically relevant not only to the Bible and the wisdom corpus but also to any and all proverbs, whatever their provenance, as long as they are of the wisdom category; that is to say, as long as they meet the two minimum requirements: they must be constituted by *two* valuational topics and they must express *comparative value.* Thus, "be strong" does not suffice because it does not have two terms, nor would statements of simple preference such as "Bill is better than John." However, "be strong and rich" does qualify when it undergoes a typical transformation such as: "it is better to be poor than weak," or, more fully: "It is better to be poor and strong than rich and weak." By the same token, proverbs offering simple advice such as weather and health proverbs also seem excluded: "An apple a day keeps the doctor away" does offer a value (apples are healthful, health is valuable) but is disqualified because in its usual performance its value is not compared.[21] Of course and as previously observed, to say that wisdom proverbs must express comparative value is tautological, since such sayings are comparative through the very fact that they are axiological. To say what is "good" or "bad" behavior is also to state or at least imply what it is "better than" or "worse than."

There is a class of better-than proverbs that seems to escape the quadripartite structure by virtue of being simple preferences or direct evaluations (Murphy 1981, 66–67, quoting RSV):

---

20. For further discussion of this topic, see the commentary to Abot 5:10–15 in the Appendix and also Chapter 3.2, "The Argument of Value."

21. Unless, of course, in performance apples are asserted to be valued above other fruits, thus creating the opposition "good food/bad food," which is then contextualized by the implied opposition, "health/sickness," suggested in this proverb by the presence of a doctor.

For the gain from it is better than gain from silver, and its profit better than gold. (Prov 3:14)

He who is slow to anger is better than the mighty, and he who rules his spirit than he who takes a city. (Prov 16:32)

A good name is to be chosen rather than great riches, and favor is better than silver or gold. (Prov 22:1)

Bryce argues (1972b, 349) that the last two can generate fuller structures; indeed, it seems to me that all such "simple" sayings of comparison are either no comparisons at all,[22] or they are regular structures such as have been studied above and thus all capable of generating fuller structures.

In the first instance, there is a formal reason why the proposition "*A* is better than *B*" is not a wisdom proverb: under the guise of a purely formalistic comparison, it merely asserts superiority and without the requisite contextualization of a second topic. This may be illustrated by the following saying: "He who cleaves to faithfulness,[23] the goodwill of his fellows cleaves to him; and he who diminishes his faithfulness increases his enemies" (*MF:*5, lines 12–13). Stylistically, this is a tautology, since the second proposition could be learned from the first, by simple negation. Note also the stylistic repetitions that reinforce the meanings: in the case of the positive value, cleaving leads to cleaving; when this pursuit of value is reversed, then "diminishing" leads to its opposite, "increase" of enemies. In terms of quadripartite structure, however, this saying expresses a simple preference, not a better-than. It simply asserts that "faithfulness is better than unfaithfulness." The friend/enemy complex is not a topic but the defining scale of value, and location on this scale will determine the relative amount of positive or negative virtue. Its function is causal and explanatory: Be faithful because it produces more friends. Note that causality is not conditional here but constitutive. We are not dealing with "faithfulness which leads to friendship," since it is assumed that all faithfulness has that result.

Although, in the previous example, faithfulness and its implied opposite constitute only one of the topics, a quadripartite can be easily constructed by introducing another topic. For example:

22. See Chapter 3.2.e, "Beyond Compare."
23. Hebr. `emunah, Sp. lealtat.

1. rich and faithful
2. poor and faithful
3. rich and unfaithful
4. poor and unfaithful

In a similar way the simple forms of Proverbs can be transformed into the usual quadripartites because they already contain the basis for the regular structures in that they all compare the (**W**isdom) topic of proposition 2 with the **w**-topic of proposition 3. Thus:

2. X and wisdom $(-+)$
3. riches and Y $(+-)$

Obviously, the implication is that X is the opposite of "riches" and Y is the opposite of "wisdom." Thus, a total structure may be generated through the comparison or, rather, contrast of the two "plus" topics. Thus: "To obey is better than sacrifice, and to hearken than the fat of lambs" (1 Sam 15:22). In restated form:

1. sacrifice and obey
2. not sacrifice and obey
3. sacrifice and not obey
4. not sacrifice and not obey

It also seems helpful to recall the initial text of Paul, which is simply the obverse wisdom form in that it compares the two negative topics $(-)$. In such a case, the topic that is "best" or beyond compare becomes the positive member of proposition 2. To be included here is the frequent formula "there is no . . . like," which often occurs in strings, as in the following: "There is no wealth like wisdom, no poverty like foolishness, etc." (*MF*:32, no. 16). Here too, although the first value is "beyond compare," this is only the better to assert its value as wisdom, as against the usual ways of the world, through the form of paradox. That wealth also has value is asserted elsewhere in the text. For example: "The best of life is in knowledge and wealth, for through these two you will be honored by both the few and the many" (*MF*:42, no. 2; cf. also 33, no. 24).

One should thus always examine the context of even simple comparisons. Take, for example, the philosopher Diogenes' assertion: "I am richer than the King of Persia" (*MF*:32, no. 22). When challenged, he explains: "I have little

and am contented; he has much and is discontented. He has worries and I don't."
Obviously, the simple comparison now discloses a typical better-than proverb:

2. poor and contented (in the present) or unworried (about the
   future)
3. rich and discontented or worried

Structurally speaking, the names "Diogenes" and "the King of Persia" are not
to be considered as topics but simply provide the commentary or interpretation of these two propositions, respectively. Interestingly, Diogenes returns
as the subject yet another time, again in the form of a paradox. This time he
is challenged by some "wealthy men," obviously in the form of a suggestion
that their life is "better than" his. His answer again applies the wisdom
predicate that reverses the values: "It is in my power to live your kind of life if
I wished, but it is not in your power to live my kind of life" (*MF:32*, no. 20).
Thus, again:

2. poor and wise (in the sense of self-control or flexibility)
3. rich and foolish

In short, while language does of course allow simple comparisons of the type
"Bill is better than John," such statements must always be carefully analyzed
to see exactly what is being asserted.

We can thus agree with Bryce that apparently simple assertions can conceal
fuller structures. Consider the original example and a similar one from the
end of the Middle Ages:

> A good name is to be chosen rather than great riches. (Prov 22:1)

> It is better to be a good mistress than a bad wife. (*La Celestina* [1969, 206])

Both texts are in fact based on topic plus attribute ("name" + "good,"
"mistress" + "good"). Thus, when placed in our valuational grid:

1. riches and good name
2. poverty and good name
3. riches and bad name
4. poverty and bad name

This typical wisdom saying, in its full meaning, asserts that fame is to be preferred even when it entails poverty. In the second text, however, "good" is itself an authentic second valuational topic:

1. good wife
2. good mistress
3. bad wife
4. bad mistress

This is a particularly interesting evaluation within the context of the play *La Celestina*, since the excluded extremities have different explanations. The woman is prevented from ever being a wife by the code of courtly love that discourages marriage (or, perhaps, by her lover, who is not seeking a wife), and she is prevented from being a "bad" mistress by her own feelings of love.

5. Variant Forms: Structural Analysis of Problem Texts

We have seen how certain variant or "broken" forms of better-than proverbs can best be understood as presupposing an underlying quadripartite model. Let us now pursue this analysis a bit further. As a preface to more problematic variations, consider the following example, taken not from a wisdom text but rather from a prophetic one: "As you have forsaken Me and served foreign gods in your own land, so shall you serve strangers in a land that is not yours" (Jer 5:19). The structure is as follows:

3. serve foreign gods in your land $(-+)$
4. serve foreigners outside of your land $(--)$

Obviously, two better possibilities exist:

1. serve God in your land
2. serve God outside of your land

The variant is that, whereas the typical comparison is between propositions 2 and 3, here it is 3 and 4 that are compared (not as better-than but rather as a resultive).

Let us now try to analyze a set of problem texts with the aid of our structural model: "To leave truth because I do not know it is better than to leave it because I hate it" (*MF*:24, no. 15). Recasting this in a conjunctive form produces the following:

1. not leave and know (> love)   (++)
2. leave and not know (> not hate)   (−+)
3. not leave and not know (> not love)   (+−)
4. leave and know? (> hate)   (−−)

The structural variant here is again that proposition 2 is stated as better-than 4 rather than 3. The explanation is that here the same behavior is being compared where the motives are different; the analogous example, taken from the same text, would produce the following: "Not to leave because I know is better than not to leave because I don't know." There seems nothing spectacular in such a position, unless it is taken as a refutation of a nonrationalist position such as "I believe because it is absurd." But the text is complicated by the dual second topic "know and love," and though it is possible to interpret proposition 4 as "to leave because of a hatred arising from ignorance," the structure imposes what seems to me a more audacious "worst of all" statement (or at least more damaging to the "truth" being advocated): "to leave because of a hatred arising from what I know."[24]

Similar to this is the following saying, cast in anecdotal form: "A man watched Socrates as he was being led to death and said to him: 'I am grieved that you are being killed through no fault of your own.' Socrates answered: 'Would you prefer that I be killed because I am at fault?'" (*MF*:21, no. 68). Thus:

1. life and not guilty   (++)
2. death and not guilty   (−+)
3. life and guilty   (+−)
4. death and guilty   (−−)

The form of the saying, however, again compares not propositions 2 and 3 but rather 2 and 4. This pattern seems to occur when the two topics (life and

24. Or, the source of the difficulty may be that better-than structures work best when the relation between topics is either conjunctive or possessive but not when it is causative, which has more affinity with equational structures.

innocence) present no clear choice between them, or perhaps when it is merely a question of cutting one's losses, of selecting or affirming what is "less bad."

Similar in structure is the following: "He is not good who does evil; rather he is good who does no evil" (*BP*:59, line 25).[25] The explanatory structure is as follows:

1. good and doing it $(++)$
2. evil and not doing it $(-+)$
3. good and not doing it $(+-)$
4. evil and doing it $(--)$

Interestingly, while the above Spanish version compares propositions 2 and 4, the Hebrew translation of the same text compares propositions 1 and 2: "The good is not when one desists from doing evil but rather when one does the good" (*MF*:32, no. 6). Neither follows the typical better-than formula, consonant with the search for what is "good" rather than for the comparative. However, each implies a comparison of sorts, or at least an approximation at defining what is good. Most curious is the redundancy of the first clause in the Spanish text, which can of course be justified as a foil preparing the main assertion. Equally plausible is the view that the redundancy is an answer to such an argument as that proposed in the Hebrew version. Thus, the Spanish text would reply, "while we can both agree that not doing evil is 'good' ... " In other words, both speakers draw their comparisons with proposition 2 and bring different answers to a terminological problem, which is: Can one call "good" the act of refraining from evil, or is that honorific term to be reserved for positive acts of goodness? Is proposition 2 a form of the good or not entirely so? In short, the differences here seem less textual than ideological. Semantically and axiologically speaking, the answers reflect two attitudes to wisdom, as well as, perhaps, crucial theological differences between the Christian Spanish text and the Jewish Hebrew one. According to the former, which believes in original sin and man's intrinsic evil, mere neutralization constitutes a "good." For the latter, for which no such dogma exists, "good" should be reserved for positive deeds, in accord with the two possibilities implied in the verse "turn from evil and do good" (Ps 34:15; 37:27). The Christian text does not claim, of course, that mere restraint is sufficient, as the text goes on to assert: "It is not sufficient for a person to desist from evil; rather we must desist from evil and do good."[26] Both

---

25. "Non es bueno el que faze el mal, mas es bueno el que non faze mal." Cf. Job 28:28.

26. "Non abonda a onbre quitarse del mal, mas dévese quitar del mal y faser el bien" (*BP*:32, line 24).

traditions seem to agree, however, that the removal of evil is better than the existence of good.

The practical counsel on self-defense, "People who live in glass houses shouldn't throw stones," generates the following:

1. stone house and don't throw
2. glass house and don't throw
3. stone house and throw
4. glass house and throw

Such a full structure obviously presupposes that the person has the choice not only to throw/not throw but also to construct his or her line of defense from stone or glass. In such a case the advice imposed by the structure is that less physical protection combined with less aggression is a "better" form of security than aggression emanating from heavy walls. Thus, proposition 2 can be compared with either proposition 3 or 4. In the latter case, it is addressed to those who live in glass houses: "Don't throw stones!" But it can also be addressed to those aggressive natures who may like to throw: "Be sure to build a stone house!"

6. Parallelism or Spurious Quadripartites

I began by distinguishing form from structure and went on to suggest ways in which different forms could be expressive of that deep structure which I have labeled quadripartite. However, I do not imply necessary connections between the two. For example, it is possible to generate spurious quadripartites, that is to say, structures of four that seem suggested by the text but which do not conform to my model. Consider, for example, Ps 97:11: "Light is sown for the righteous, and joy for the upright of heart." One wonders whether it is being proposed that the righteous have no joy in store for them? Or, again:

1. The wise son brings gladness to his father,
2. and the foolish son brings anguish to his mother. (Prov 10:1)

Can this possibly suggest that the wise son does not also cause his mother to rejoice, or that the foolish son does not also bring anguish to his father?

It is much more likely that, in a typical performance, this pair of propositions was seen as implying two others as well (Menachem ha-Meiri 1969, 84):

> 1a. The wise son causes his mother to rejoice.
> 2a. The foolish son brings anguish upon his father.

Why then not state this as well? Perhaps simply because this binary or parallelistic pattern is the peculiar style of many biblical proverbs. On the one hand they say too little; on the other, even this binary is too much, since the second proposition can usually be generated from the first (but not by opposition, as is usually the case; see below, this section). This concern to escape both overexplicitness and oversuccinctness strikes me as a valid explanation of the binary statement verse-form of the Book of Proverbs, especially chapters 10–15. We should acknowledge, however, that this instance of "two that are four"[27] is primarily a literary device; it does not give any new knowledge or insight. This is not to dispute the Rabbis' refusal of parallelism, but rather to observe that, *structurally* as well as semantically speaking, parallelistic verses can be conflated. Thus, Prov 10:1 asserts, and in accord with Menachem ha-Meiri:

> 1. the wise son causes his parents to rejoice. $(++)$
> 2. the foolish son brings anguish upon both. $(--)$

It may be, however, that ha-Meiri goes out of his way to insist on this point for structural as well as semantic reasons, not only to assert his own valuation of the proverb but also to counter the unconscious tendency to put all such sayings on a quadripartite grid. For obviously, through the usual procedures of opposition, two further statements can also be generated:

> 3. the wise son brings anguish upon his parents.
> 4. the foolish son causes them to rejoice.

While from a wisdom perspective such views seem absurd, the problem here may be that we have an unconscious habit of reading such statements as definitional, in which case they are indeed absurd. That is to say, we understand "a wise son" to be precisely "one who causes his parents to rejoice." That such a standard cannot be regarded as always definitional could be

---

27. This tag is taken from Rabbinic discourse; as an example, cf. Mishnah Shabbat 1:1.

illustrated by the case of Esau, whose ability to bring joy to his father Isaac may not be regarded as proof of his excellence as an offspring (Gen 25:19f.).[28]

A related issue has to do with the wisdom habit of noticing or reading topics as oppositional. Take once more ha-Meiri's other proof-text: "Light is sown for the righteous, and joy for the upright of heart" (Ps 97:11). It would seem to be pushing a structural point beyond acceptable limits to read "joy and light" or "righteous and upright" as oppositional, and this is why ha-Meiri, perhaps correctly, objects. One could claim, however, that even here the method applies and, indeed, is encouraged by the text. As against ha-Meiri, let us read this in the usual way:

1. joy for the righteous $(++)$
2. light for the righteous $(-+)$
3. joy for the upright of heart $(+-)$
4. light for the upright of heart $(--)$

The usual translation would then have to be revised: "Light is sown for the righteous, but for the upright of heart there is present joy." The point would be Kohelet's, that *simhah* or joy in the present is to be preferred to a less tangible "light," and this higher reward is reserved to the "righteous" *doers* rather than the merely upright "of heart."

28. One could of course debate many of these points, notably whether Esau's service to his father can in any way be considered as a sign of his unworthiness (one would rather propose that, at least from this evidence, he was a good son). From an exegetical point of view, in the discussion of Prov 10:1 one would want to ask whether it is in fact true that a wise or foolish child causes *both* parents joy or grief and whether it is therefore legitimate to spell out the implications of the verse. Again, the example of Esau and Jacob could be brought forth in refutation, since neither child can convince *both* parents (Gen 25:28). One of the points of the verse, therefore, would be precisely that each parent has different sensitivities and that the reactions of neither can be considered as proof. Thus, it would be more likely, according to Prov 10:1, for a foolish son to bring anguish to the mother rather than the father, as illustrated in the sequel to the same story (Gen 28:46).

3

THE WISDOM OF STRUCTURE

In this chapter we pass to the message of wisdom, to the values that the sages sought to transmit and instill. Many excellent studies have already been devoted to this theme, and I have no wish to repeat their work. Rather, I would like to pursue my own method by asking what wisdom values are implicit in the structural approach itself as outlined above. If it is true, as I have argued, that historical quadripartites—the full or explicit ones but also the broken or partial ones as well—are a particular contribution of wisdom to the world of proverbs, what values does this imply? We pass, then, to wisdom's principles or values as expressed in its structures and structural analyses rather than its specific message or content.

1. The Limitations of Proverbs
and Their Structures

(A) THE AUTHORITY OF PROVERBS

Despite the difficulty of defining proverbs, we are quite convinced we can recognize them. Indeed, their brevity, their frequent recourse to rhyme ("Haste makes waste") and alliteration ("Look before you *leap*"), our very ponderous manner of presenting proverbs through interruption of the syntagmatic line (there is a list of consecrated formulas such as "as the saying goes," "as they say") or a knowing change of tone—these aspects of their normal appearance point to a more decisive feature, their presumption of *authority*. According to James L. Crenshaw, proverbs seem to "encapsulate truth" (1981, 68). Similarly, John Mark Thompson (1974, 23; cited in Crenshaw 1981, 68) observes that, upon hearing a proverb for the first time, "it is as though, within the depths of human consciousness, we perceive the proverb's content to be true."

If truth is characteristic of proverbs, however, then what are we to think of such sayings as the following: "Stolen waters are sweet, and bread eaten in secret is pleasant" (Prov 9:17). The message is made yet more enticing by the careful balance of stress (three in each member) and the internal rhyme:

> *máyim genubím yimtáqu / we-léḥem setarím yin ʿám.*
> Waters stolen are sweet / and bread hidden is pleasant.

Yet, in the Book of Proverbs this proverb is used by a whore to seduce an unwary youth! We now understand the condensed or poetic form of such sayings a bit better, for their intent is not only mnemonic but also persuasive and even a bit incantatory, what Havelock (1963) ascribed to the monologism of the poets of Greece preceding the Socratic introduction of critical thinking.

Closely allied with proverbs' presumption of authority is their anonymity and popular appeal: they are typically spoken in the eternal present ("stolen waters *are* sweet") and their source is anonymous (everyone can't be wrong!). But despite their appearance of *consensus,* they are tyrannically single-voiced, typically used to win conviction rather than to gain insight, to clinch and end an argument, not continue one or provoke another. Note also the deceptive observational tone of this saying, which seeks to persuade and teach a mode of conduct not by the traditional exhortations of moral didacticism but rather by appeal to experiential "truth."

Through their use of moral commonplace and platitudes, proverbs are thus one of the best ploys of automatic thinking and monologism. In addition to a specific message, proverbs celebrate consensus for its own sake. They are thus highly dangerous in the wrong hands, as the whore in Proverbs reminds us, and this is why they are used with such caution by the sages. In the text under discussion, for example, these normal presumptions of proverbs, their authority and consensus, are deconstructed or neutralized by the wisdom writer before being presented. Thus, the whore's proverb of seduction is carefully framed by the following preface: "And to him who is without sense she said" [RSV: "she says"]. RSV's disregard of the past "she said" in favor of the present "she says" follows the general impulse of such sayings toward the eternal present, but in so doing it jeopardizes the neutralizing effect of wisdom's *anti*formulaic presentation, in clear contrast to the usual "as *they* say." Through this presentation the wisdom writer destroys any illusion of eternal present and truth by localizing the event as a single incident in the past, thus emphasizing that its author is not the voice of consensus but only a seductress.

In daily life one is struck by such propagandistic uses of proverbs, the exemplary form of which I have already labeled proverbs of simple preference: "X tastes better," "we try harder," "better dead than red," and the like. That this is not a purely modern occurrence can be seen from older examples already cited: "haste makes waste," "stolen waters are sweet," etc. Advertising, whether commercial or political or religious, has brought these upon us like a plague, like the hucksters that swarm at my front door or on my telephone line. Whether precise definition of such impostures is indeed impossible, as Archer Taylor (1931) would have it, it is at least agreed that their style has a proverbial ring, and such tricks as their brevity and rhyme seem geared more to foreclose on analysis rather than provoke it. However, such examples do not bespeak the universality of proverbs but rather of authority. The child who scrambles to the top of the haystack and claims to be the "king of the mountain," the usurper who rises above the heap of opponents and proclaims that "might makes right": these learn that language, and all the more so proverbs, is a tool of authority, that the pen can indeed be mightier than the sword! But opponents soon learn that swords defend against swords, and so it is with pens and proverbs.

Protection against such aggression is not always so easy as disconnecting the phone, refusing to answer the doorbell, or defacing bumper-stickers. I am far from insisting that humanity is doomed to be victimized by proverbial assertions until more sages come along to protect us, for just as bodies generate antibodies, popular wisdom gives rise to its own protectants. For example, some languages have built-in safeguards. Modern French, for example, will not allow such a construction as "we try harder," for the second term of the comparative must be specified: "We try harder *than Y.*" Even in English these are recognized as false comparisons, in reality unverifiable superlatives: "We try harder than everyone else!" Another protective reaction is to cite or generate a counterproverb, either from the same elements (e.g., "Better red than dead!") or in direct contradiction. Consider the following sequence:

> Do not answer a fool according to his folly,
>   lest you become like him yourself.
> Answer a fool according to his folly,
>   lest he be wise in his own eyes.
>   (Prov 26:4–5)

It is well known that such *contradictory proverbs* exist in large numbers in all proverb traditions. When I pointed this out to a native Ladino speaker, a culture with a high incidence of such contradictory proverbs, the reply was: "Of course, that's the way it has to be!"

The role of contradictories must be examined a bit further, since it has been plausibly proposed that what characterizes proverbs is precisely the flexible role they play in a culture's belief system. Take, for example, the two following sentences (Cram 1983, 53–54):

> Nicotine makes the heart beat faster.

> Absence makes the heart grow fonder.

If each is contradicted, then very different consequences follow. In the first case, it is true either that

> Nicotine makes the heart beat faster

or

> Nicotine makes the heart beat slower.

However, both cannot be true (or false) at the same time. By contrast, consider the following:

Absence makes the heart grow fonder.

Out of sight, out of mind.

It is thus possible that, within different circumstances, *both* contradictory proverbs can be true (or false).

The mere existence of contradictory proverbs within a given proverb system, it must be stressed, proves only that a particular existential situation *can* provoke several different reactions or interpretations; here it is the application or performative interpretation that is decisive. It is therefore necessary to distinguish two scenarios. First, take the case of the simple assertion "out of sight, out of mind." This proverb of simple preference can be countered, in performance, by the contradictory "absence makes the heart grow fonder." This series might generate further proverbial debate, and it is precisely the ongoing contestation that approximates, through the very citation of "popular" proverbs," what is here termed a wisdom function.

Second, Kirshenblatt-Gimblett (1981, 112–13) has explained the multiple and even contradictory interpretations of the same proverb within the same culture (e.g., the famous case of "a rolling stone gathers no moss"). The existence of such proverbs is a mere fact of life, witness to the flexibility of proverbs and the complexity of both existential situations and language. It is only when, as before, these contradictories are brought in performative conflict, when other participants are made aware of the multiple possibilities of interpretation, that the sage's (in this case the investigator herself) *wisdom* function is simulated.

But the more traditional and far-ranging precaution against the authoritarianism of proverbs is simple skepticism and analysis, perhaps in the form of a question, whereupon the authority of such slogans vanishes like smoke: "you try harder than who?" "Does haste always make waste?" "Is it always better to marry?" (cf. Kirshenblatt-Gimblett 1981, 115). Although such contestation is not limited to proverbs, this genre has established itself historically as a natural focus of such activity, and in this study I try to distinguish the initial, authoritarian, or "natural" use of proverbs from those sayings and techniques that hold them in check. The first assert; the second contest the first (e.g., through critical analysis) or propose alternatives. To the degree that a history of monologism versus dialogism is possible, it is also possible to trace the origins and practices of two proverb traditions. I have rather boldly proposed the name "popular" for the first, but the second can be called by its traditional name: wisdom. It thus becomes possible, as I proposed in the Introduction, that by using these concepts as polar opposites, to study the development and inner dynamic of proverbs in their wisdom function. To the question, then, as to why we need wisdom sayings in the first place, tradition replies not only at the level of Doxa or of morality but also of awareness of the nature of language and the importance of critical thinking. Thus, one could imagine that the entire Book of Kohelet, for example, was written to undo the totalizing assertion that "all is vanity,"[1] and Dame Wisdom's aphorisms in the Book of Proverbs have as their goal to refute not only the wiles of the "stranger woman" but also her speech, her "coaxing words," that aphoristically seek to persuade that "stolen waters are sweet" (Williams 1981, 25). This would imply a dynamic and dialogic or *contestatory* use of proverbs, an approach well characterized by Santob de Carrión: "To pursue an argument with books is worth more than peace. The more one engages in tenacious dispute with books, the more good knowledge he will continue to acquire" (Santob, lines 1247–52). To aspire to dialogue with books is to grant that even books can have the last word, but especially to assert that no last word is desirable. From this perspective, the negation or opposition or contestation such as one finds in contradictory proverbs but also and especially in the very binary structure of proverbs is to be considered the very soul of wisdom proverbs; its quintessential form would be something like a debate entirely in proverbs. That is in fact what occurs in "primitive" societies or, as I argue elsewhere (1993), in the finest examples of the wisdom genre such as Kohelet.

(B) WISDOM'S SELF–CRITIQUE (KOH 9:14–10:1)

Just as proverbs can be dangerous, structure too, as traditionally conceived, has its potential weaknesses, and if the wisdom tradition can be defined as a critical one, then one can rightfully expect a healthy round of self-criticism. That is in fact what happens in Koh 9:14–10:1, which in a self-conscious way sets out to question and perhaps deconstruct the very formulas at the base of proverb construction.

---

1. Such assertions as *"all is vanity"* seem more valuable as pedagogical provocations or literary lamentations than as serious observation spoken by a reputable sage, and Maimonides does not hesitate to ascribe such complaints to ignorance (*Guide,* part III, chap. 12), with reference not to Kohelet, of course, but rather to the "ignorant followers of Al-Farabi."

The text begins with a brief narrative: "There was a small city with few inhabitants, and a great king came upon it and surrounded it with a powerful siege. There happened to be there a lowly sage and he saved the city through his wisdom" (Koh 9:14–15). The purpose of the ensuing discussion is to evaluate the meaning of this exemplum, and the main point is spoken, or at least summarized, by proverbs (Perry 1987a). In other words, what is embryonically present in this text is a "debate in proverbs," a proverb string whose coherence is dialogic. Of course, here the elements of the string are both shown to derive from the narrative and are explicitly related one to another, thus making this text all the more valuable as an example of what such strings may originally have looked like before they were stripped and anthologized.

The meaning of the tale is now advanced, in the form of a rather traditional wisdom assertion: "Wisdom is better than strength" (Koh 9:16). Implying here the simple **W**isdom preference that "Wisdom is better than foolishness," the text contextualizes the **W**isdom value with a **w**orldly value, might. This explicit contextualization enables us to see more precisely the opposite of "might," already suggested by the binary "lowly sage," now understood as physically weak and poor. The full structure can now be stated as follows:

1. strong and wise
2. lowly (weak, poor) but wise   = the sage
3. strong but foolish   = the invading king
4. lowly and foolish

In fact, the qualification "less wise, unwise, foolish" is not only implicit in the structure but also spelled out in the narrative, since this great king is outsmarted by the sage.

The interesting point about this example from Kohelet is that this traditional better-than situation is now deconstructed, and in two distinct stages. First, its initial assumption is questioned, for perhaps the form of the statement is too general: You imply that "wisdom is better," but for whom? For if wisdom is expressed by a lowly person, it is not even heard! "The poor man's wisdom is scorned [i.e., by the populace]" (Koh 9:16). The hidden supposition or prejudice of the first formulation is now uncovered, for when it is spelled out it is seen as referring only to the sage (or to the opposite, the unwise king), and it asserts that wisdom (or its lack) is good (or bad) for them. But what about the real victims, the few inhabitants of the small city, since in the context now being proposed there are not two parties—the sage and the king—but three, the third being the besieged people themselves?

Here the objection addresses the usual situation in the world: people don't hear or don't listen to advice when it is not properly packaged.

This critique leads to two results. First of all, the original formulation "wisdom is better than might" is exposed for what it is, a limited and unwarranted generalization. Second, a reformulation is now offered, the initial topic receives a new context: "Wisdom is better than weapons of war [i.e., of the inhabitants]" (Koh 9:18). No less than the first proverb, the second is also formulated as a proverb of simple preference. The point here, it seems to me, is the reverse of what we have found to be the case. I have argued that all better-than sayings imply a context, meaning that even proverbs of simple preference are usually quadripartites in disguise. Kohelet now reverses the point: all quadripartites, even explicit ones, are really proverbs of simple preference in that they simply and without proof assert one value over another. Thus, in these two instances wisdom is successively asserted to be better than (a) the strength of the invading king, and (b) the arms of the defenders. Still, the new formula has a very different perspective or context, or rather it emphasizes different elements in the source narrative: Wisdom, even unarmed, is better than foolishness, even armed. The stress is now on the objectively vulnerable and defenseless situation of the besieged city. This shift in perspective from that of the perpetrator to that of the victim runs counter to classical notions of ethics (cf. Perry 1987b, 135). This passage from Kohelet affords a rare glimpse into the kind of critical discussion that must have been normal procedure in wisdom gatherings.

The critique now takes a radical turn, however, since it is leveled not only against the context and the assertion of value but also against the very basis of the structure, against the value "good" implied in the standard formula "better than." The text takes on this rather bold argument through a play on words:

"Wisdom is better (*tobah*, good) than weapons of war."

"But one fool can destroy much good" (*tobah*).[2] (Koh 9:18)

If "good" is now seen as "not so good," the text is obliged to invent a new formula, fashioned according to the traditional and recognizable one but with a shift or reversal of values: "A little foolishness is *weightier* than [not 'better than'] wisdom, than honor" (Koh 10:1). What is questioned here is both the prime value of the wisdom tradition—wisdom itself—and the very

2. For the wordplay see Gordis (1968, 312–13).

value of "better-than" through which it asserts itself; although wisdom may indeed have value, it is not necessarily preferable even to foolishness.[3]

(C) THREE THAT ARE (OR ARE NOT) FOUR

Among wisdom's formulas is a construction that may be termed *three that are four* (e.g., Prov 30:15, 18, 21, 29).[4] In a wisdom context it could also be called *three that are not four,* since it focuses on the Excluded Fourth by considering the exception that tests the rule. For example, from Juan Manuel's observation that there is such a thing as "bad truth"[5] one can infer the following structure:

1. the good (truth) is good
2. the bad is bad
3. the good is bad
4. the bad is good

The first two are givens, required to be asserted by moralists, nevertheless, because of the deceptions of daily experience, the *engaños* that are so prevalent in Old Spanish literature. Thus, the prophet asserts that "Out of the wicked comes forth wickedness" (1 Sam 24:14, E13). Proposition 3, Juan Manuel's example "bad truth," is more difficult to situate but can in fact be exemplified in experience: it is bad, for example, to overpraise a good person in his presence. The fourth proposition, however, is, according to Juan Manuel at least, never true. The most that he will concede is, in our first sample text, that evil may at times *seem* to be good. But he insists that "wrong is wrong"[6] and thus, by implication, that the structure is mislead-

---

3. Again, the context is crucial to interpretation:

"One fool can destroy much good."

Dead flies can spoil an entire container of perfumer's ointment, causing it to stink.
(Koh 9:18–10:1)

Thus, even if it is not questioned whether wisdom is "better" or a better value, the real issue in human life is rather the removal of negative values, which thus turn out to be weightier. For further examples of this important point see Chapter 3.2.c, "Relative Value."

4. The formula also occurs in prophetic texts, such as the long series at the start of Amos.

5. "[v]erdat mala" *Lucanor* 448, line 132.

6. "El yerro es yerro" *Lucanor* 458, line 123.

ing. What is a limitation from one perspective becomes a challenge from another, however; when confronted with the commentary or interpretation of "the bad is good," the Rabbis gave the example of the permissibility of lying in order to bring peace.[7]

It can thus happen that a sense of the structure (of all the logical possibilities of combination of the terms) allows the generation of a proposition (the excluded fourth) that is striking because of its absurdity or conundrumlike challenge to logic or sense. For how, for example, can one fall into a grave that is not even dug? Yet Karl Kraus can assert that "Who digs no grave for another falls in it himself" (cited in Williams 1981, 13). Structurally this aphorism can be analyzed as but one of the logical possibilities suggested by Prov 26:27: "He who digs a pit will fall into it":[8]

1. doesn't dig and doesn't fall
2. digs and falls
3. digs and doesn't fall
4. doesn't dig and falls!

Here the specifications "grave" and "for another" are merely contextual, part of the interpretation rather than the structure. The important point is that Kraus is poking fun at the structural possibilities, and we smile because we too are aware of these (absurd but perhaps morally real) possibilities.

(D) HUMOR AND RIDDLELIKE QUESTIONS

Given both the abstract and general nature of many such propositions, the search for appropriate contexts in which they are true becomes so speculative and difficult as to suggest affinities with riddles. Indeed, the addition of a commentary to the basic structure points to what must have been the expected practice in such exercises: to guess the context in which such paradoxes are true and to specify the extent of such contexts. Here the "feeling of release" (Milner 1969b, 380) comes first from the amusement at

7. Some even allowed flattery of the wicked, as having survival value. For example, Santob (lines 543–44) requires one to honor a bad man in order to be "protected from his evil." From a structural point of view it may be assumed that, although the complete quadripartite is not stated as such and has to be reconstructed in such texts and value systems, it can be assumed to be operative when, at other junctures, the text makes valuations that assume the reconstructed statements (see Milner 1969b, 382).

8. Cf. also Koh 10:8; Ps 7:16 E15.

being presented with a possibility that seems only logical, imposed by the structure, and remote from experience; and then from the discovery of the answer.

An excellent example is the following, because it states a previous saying in riddle form:

> What is true but not good?
>
> [Answer] Boasting.[9]

Another text begins with the common moral premise that in all things value is in inverse proportion to amount possessed, with the result that

> 1. more is less
> 2. less is more

The riddle thus takes the following rather paradoxical form:

> When is more more and less less? (propositions 3 and 4, implied in the structure)
>
> [Answer] In *saber*, knowledge. (*Flores de filosofía* [1878, 36 n. 1])

As a final example, recall one previously cited:

> When is a friend an enemy?
>
> [Answer] When he is the friend of an enemy.

Or:

> When is an enemy a friend?
>
> [Answer] When he is an enemy of an enemy.

Humor is not always kind or merely playful or enigmatic, however, and an appeal to structure can expose darker uses of popular proverbs. In his seminal studies, Milner (1969b, 382) provided what he considers the more basic form of the proverb. Here is an example:

9. ¿Quál es la cosa que non es buena maguer sea verdat? (*Bocados de oro* 1879, 183, lines 27–31).

> Those who speak don't know;
> those who know don't speak.

Milner suggests that each of these lines is a macroproverb, but that both are required for the release of humor, as well as for the high mnemonic value, both peculiar to proverbs. This doubling is consistent with my own experience of the following proverb: "A woman's work is never done," which always has impressed me by its truth but never aesthetically until I heard it joined to its first part:

> A man works from sun to sun,
> but a woman's work is never done.

I would like to suggest, however, that even the extended form of the basic proverb is itself only a macroproverb or saying, dependent upon an unspoken (and perhaps only unconsciously perceived) but logically required second half. Thus, the complete saying implied in the above is as follows:

1. Those who speak know;
2. Those who don't speak don't know;
3. Those who speak don't know;
4. Those who know don't speak.

This form, which is the one suggested by the language, is one of cause and result, close to the equational structure. The weakness of this structure is that it excludes the first two members under guise of exclusivity. In order to produce a structure more true to experience, therefore, this equational structure has to be restated in conjunctive form:

1. there are those who speak and know
2. there are those who don't speak and don't know
3. there are those who speak and don't know
4. there are those who know and don't speak.

The first two members, I would argue, are as true to experience as the second two. In a typical proverbial or "popular" reading, however, they are slyly disregarded (or, perhaps, concealed through an equational structure), with the connivance of the audience, producing a truncated version of reality much like jokes about women or ethnics, which enforce a vision of a part for the whole. The "reversal of normal values" (Milner 1969b, 382) that produces amusement is thus based on a willfully partial or prejudiced version of reality accepted with audience complicity. The original proverb, therefore, whether of one or two propositions, must be considered as derivative from the original quadripartite (conjunctive) structure; the normally humorous but hurtful reading is overcome, in a wisdom reading, by insisting on inclusion of the remaining elements of structure.[10]

A variant of this structure may offer further clarification. Referring to the progress of argumentative discourse in a discourse unit such as John 3:1–21, Daniel Patte (1990a, 14) describes the *inverted parallelism* that exists between introduction and conclusion: "there is parallelism because both deal with the same theme; this parallelism is inverted because the introduction presents the theme as problematic, while the conclusion presents it as a resolved issue." Analogously, it seems possible to propose that proverbs of the type AB/BA are inverted parallelisms in which the argument (analogous, in Patte's example, to the body of the narrative) has been suppressed. Take, for example, the case of translations, which is also connivingly referred to women:

1. If they are beautiful they are not faithful.
2. If they are faithful they are not beautiful.

Milner (1969b, 382) observes that if the first proposition alone is stated, "it does not arouse laughter, or at least amusement, and does not even arouse interest." This is indeed surprising, since one could easily infer proposition 2 from the first. However, if only proposition 1 is stated, it has the character of a mere assertion; whereas if the second is added, then the entire saying takes on the character of an argument with an ironclad conclusion. In other words, in smiling one participates in the contrivance of willfully suppressing the body of the argument itself, which would include two further propositions of analysis:

10. Parenthetically, in the first pair of our example, the "and" is conjunctive and perhaps also causative: they speak because they know and don't speak because they don't know. In the second pair, the "and" is adversative ("and" means "but"): they speak although they don't know; they know although they don't speak. Although this seems the "wisdom" reading, a more humorous reading can be had by introducing the causative meaning into the second pair: They speak because they don't know (speech being a substitute for their emptiness), and they know because they don't speak (viewing speech either as a hindrance to certain kinds of knowledge, or simply reckoning the time saved by silence as applied to further learning). There is of course a further reason for the release of humor in this saying: the pessimistic and ironic statement of the *worse* is followed by the *next to worse*.

> If they are beautiful they are faithful.
> If they are not beautiful they are not faithful.

Rather than pausing to consider these possibilities as well, the listener is rushed to the conclusion, precipitously enforced by a chiastic structure that closes the door on reflection and proposes its truth as obvious. Thus, introduction and conclusion—the problem and its obvious solution—occupy the entire space of argument, and this appearance of inclusive certitude makes us restful and satisfied. And, when it is at another's expense, as here, the "truth" arouses humor, that "feeling of release and amusement" (Milner 1969b, 380).

(E) WHAT'S WHAT? ($X = X$?): THE DECEPTIONS OF LANGUAGE

In the study of equational proverbs in Chapter 2, I concluded with a question: If "cheap is [really] expensive" and "enough is [really] too much," then why not say so? In other words, why are equationals needed at all? What is the nature of the disguise and implied paradox of equational structures? It was observed that the tensions produced by the structure, here the identical-looking second topic, force an awareness of ambivalence and a search for new meanings and accommodations. We have just seen how such structures can be used humorously to conceal the (better part of the) truth. Let us pursue this matter of ambivalence a bit further.

For the sake of experiment, let us construct a typical quadripartite by applying the usual procedures. Let us begin with any topic, say, "winning." Since the opposite is "losing," the following structure can be generated:

1. he who wins wins[11] $(++)$
2. he who loses loses $(--)$
3. he who wins loses $(+-)$
4. he who loses wins. $(-+)$

While, from the point of view of pure logic, propositions 1 and 3 cannot coexist, in proverbs the laws of normal logic do not apply and one can easily imagine concrete applications of each.[12] Thus, "he who wins wins (nevertheless)," in reply to one who tries to minimize the victory. On the other

---

11. The logical connective "is" is often omitted in equational structures, as in the elliptical "marriage—torture"; "vieillesse, tristesse" (Rothstein 1968, 265–67).

12. Cf. Cram (1983); also Chapter 3.1.a, on contradictory proverbs.

hand, as wisdom writers often pointed out, in a situation in which one tries to argue with a fool and perhaps loses his temper in the process, then "he who wins loses," since even a victory is a loss.[13]

What has been achieved in both cases, by the equational as well as the oppositional proverbs, is a triumph over appearances. This triumph is achieved, moreover, by a deliberate stretching of the possibilities of language, what could be termed almost a misuse: on the one hand, by stating what logic holds to be perfectly obvious (identity); on the other, by asserting a paradox in the form of a logical contradiction.

Roland Barthes's (1972) brilliant analysis of the maxims of La Rochefoucauld brings this into sharper focus. The most typical of La Rochefoucauld's observations is cast in what Barthes calls "the relation of deceptive identity." For example,

> La clémence des princes *n'est* souvent *qu*'une politique pour gagner l'affection des peuples.

> The clemency of princes *is* often *only* a political trick to win over the affection of subject peoples. (emphasis added)

The aphorist's task is to unmask the underlying identity of clemency and "politique," and his stylistic ploy is the reductive *n'est que,* which reveals an altruistic appearance as "only" self-interest. And, like all equational structures, "it doesn't explain, it defines" (76): this is what clemency really is![14]

The definition proceeds in opposite paths, however; if La Rochefoucauld "defines the more (the appearance) by the less (the real)," wisdom writers redefine the lesser topic (the **w**-value) by appending a positive attribute, the **W**-value. One is allowed to be humble, for example, "only if . . . " Thus, "be the tail (lowly appearance) only if it is the tail of a lion"; "you may marry," says Saint Paul, "but only if it reduces desire."

From this it appears that, although La Rochefoucauld is also the observer of the deceptiveness of appearances, his disenchantment reveals him to be a spokesman (not an advocate) not for wisdom but for the usual ways of the world. Structurally, his equational formulas serve as reminders that all such topics are not equivalences but valuational (usually in their second position) and that each valuational topic can have an eroded underside or history,

13. For contrary advice on ways of dealing with fools, see Prov 26:4–5 and Hoglund (1987).

14. Beaujot (1984) refers to this aspect in his suggestive title, "Le Travail de la définition dans quelques maximes de La Rochefoucauld."

which it will be the task of sages to correct. Thus, to take up a typical Juan Manuelian formulation: "virtues are Virtues only if..." Thus the sages practice one of their most important missions, which is to purify daily language by restoring its valuational function, and especially its wisdom value.

2. The Argument of Value

One can learn from the examples already studied that, whether one argues "better than" (tob min, thus "what is good, valuable") or "weightier than" or some other valuation such as "more precious than," the point remains that *values* are being presented and evaluated, and this is in fact an important working hypothesis: Wisdom transmits values. This issue was clearly formulated in Kohelet and remained central to the wisdom enterprise (Zimmerli 1933, 176): "what is the benefit to man?" (Koh 1:3; RSV: "what does man gain"); "what is good for man while he lives" (Koh 6:12). One could even model such a perception on a spectrum: at one extreme would be Camus's *homme absurde,* who would be considered the archetypical fool since he sees no value in anything (Fox 1989, 14). In the middle would be normal people, who usually see value in terms of their own being, here and now. At the opposite extreme would be the sage, who sees value in everything—of course, in its proper time and place, since "there is no person who does not have his time, there is no thing which does not have its place" (Abot 4:3).

The argument of value is generally admitted only as applied to certain categories of wisdom statements such as the instruction, or didactic and learned sayings, but exception is often taken concerning pure observations. As an example, Murphy (1981, 4) offers the following: "One man pretends to be rich, yet has nothing; another pretends to be poor, yet has great wealth" (Prov 13:7). According to Murphy this paradox is "merely experiential." On the contrary, I propose that the example under discussion projects values in two ways: (a) from the wisdom perspective it points out a common form of deception, and it can therefore be classified as a "warning-saying"; (b) more important perhaps, the observation does not project a Wisdom value but its antagonist; it takes note of one of the "values of this world," which therefore has its own value, however limited, and which it is the task of wisdom to expose and combat. It is, in brief, a necessary foil to wisdom perspectives.

Thus, although values presented in wisdom contexts such as the Book of

Proverbs need not always be **W**isdom values and are often of a **w**orldly nature, pragmatic concerns are also of interest to wisdom writers and also imply value. One must realize, too, that proverbs not only propose actions but also "attempt to produce an attitude towards a situation that may well call for inaction and resignation" (Abrahams 1972, 121; see also Krikmann 1985, 58). For example, a proverb that attempts to create irony concerning the lazy or indifference toward the cruel is no less valuational for all its observational tone.

(A) BETTER THAN WHAT? $(+ - $ OR $ - +?)$

The argument of value can be discussed further by introducing at this point a second hypothesis or working principle: all values are either positive or negative—there are no neutral values—and can thus be symbolized by *plus* and *minus*. As in the so-called parallelism of biblical poetry, proverbs are typically binary, made up of two parts, and these can be frequently characterized as *contrary* values (plus versus minus). Thus, it is easy to assign values to such a series as Prov 10–15, with its sharply antithetical contrasts between the righteous and the wicked. Before discussing the research value of such designations, let us first consider a remarkable proof-text, the grand ode to destiny that occurs at the start of chapter 3 of Kohelet. Working from these understandings and methods, a truly significant compositional structure exists in this text, a chiasmus of plus and minus values that totally accounts for the order of verses.[15] I would like to spell out some of the implications of this structure. First, it is important to identify the oppositional values according to plus and minus. Loader (1986) himself fluctuates between calling these "favorable and unfavorable," on the one hand, and viewing them as merely descriptive on the other.

Second, it is crucial to notice the *sequence* of values in each statement: $(- +)$ or $(+ -)$. More precisely and in the very language of the text (Koh 7:8): Is the end of a thing better than its beginning? Can human life be described as:

$$- > +$$

or is the reverse true:

---

15. This structure was first pointed out by Loader (1986, 33–35); I discuss it further in my *Dialogues with Kohelet*.

$$+ > -$$

This splendid text is structured in two series of statements, chiastically arranged: the first describes what I call the way of nature or of the world, which is the decline from a life-enhancing "plus" value to its "minus" or opposite; the second series reverses the order and offers a Wisdom perspective, namely that things can get better, if only "in the long run."

A) Natural Patterns: $(+ > -)$
1. born and die (3:2)
2. plant and uproot (3:2)

7. have intercourse and abstain (3:5)
8. embrace and hold from embraces (3:5)

9. seek and give up (3:6)
10. keep and cast off (3:6)

13. love and hate (3:8)

B) Human Patterns: $(- > +)$
3. kill and heal (3:3)
4. wreck and build (3:3)

5. weep and laugh (3:4)
6. mourn and dance (3:4)

11. tear and repair (3:7)
12. be silent and speak (3:7)

14. war and peace (3:8)

The rigid chiasmus of supporting examples is 2-4-4-2, the only break occurring at the end, presumably as the reverse parallel of the opening "born and die" and also because it is better to end a series on a positive note, as noted in our study of Abot 5:15 (see Appendix). By natural-versus-human patterns I do not mean that the first series refers to nature's activities, since both series refer to the human sphere. But in the first, man's activities conform to natural patterns and the progression from $(+)$ to $(-)$ is thus irreversible: pleasure always ends up in pain, rise always leads to fall, life is relentlessly destroyed and nothing remains. The second or human series, by contrast, illustrates a paradoxical reversal of natural determinism that might properly be termed a central wisdom value.

(B) VALUE AS A COMPOSITIONAL DEVICE?

Generations of readers of such collections as Proverbs 10–29 have experienced persistent frustration over the lack of sequence, the absence of unifying patterns, indeed the solipsism, so to speak, of each verse unto itself (cf. Hildebrandt 1988). On the model of Koh 3:2–8, I would like to propose the patterned alternation of plus and minus units as a fruitful possibility for compositional research.

As found to be the case with quadripartite structures, here too earlier disciples of the sages can be of help. Such an approach was in fact suggested by Menachem ha-Meiri (1969, 23):

> [This second section (chaps. 10–24)] is not ordered in sequential portions like the first [chaps. 1–9]; rather it is all composed of separate verses with no linkages or gradations from one to the other except one of proximity. Each verse has its own subject matter, except that a verse can occasionally be related to the preceding or following verse. This second section is ordered according to four principles. The first is when a verse introduces two different subjects, praise for the praiseworthy and the opposite for the opposite. For example, "The memory of the righteous is a blessing, but the name of the wicked will rot" (v. 10:7); "a wise son makes a glad father, but a foolish man despises his mother" (v. 15:20). And most verses follow this order, from the start until v. 15:20. . . . The second principle is when the entire verse treats a single topic. For example: "He whose ear heeds wholesome admonition will abide among the wise (15:31). . . . The third principle deals with two topics, but both offer praise: "The fear of the Lord is instruction in wisdom, and humility goes before honor" (15:33). The fourth principle deals with two topics also, but both offer blame: "A perverse man spreads strife, and a whisperer separates close friends" (16:28).

One need only replace "praise and blame" by the symbols "+" and "–"; and while it is clear that not all verses conform to such patterns, large sections of the Book of Proverbs do seem to be organized in accordance with these structures. Note carefully that here I extend the "plus" and "minus" so that they characterize no longer the two individual topics (or their opposites) that make up a cola but rather the entire cola.[16] Consider, for example, Prov 10:1–4:

> A wise son makes a father glad;   (+)
> a foolish son is a sorrow to his mother.   (–)

16. Van Leeuwen (1988, 48) made a beginning in this kind of analysis when he characterized Prov 26:1–3, 6–12 as all sayings having a (– –) structure. This would correspond to ha-Meiri's fourth principle, and Van Leeuwen may therefore be imposing too severe restrictions in limiting this kind of analysis to parallelistic lines in which both colas are either plus or minus, thus yielding lines of the same value.

Treasures gained by wickedness do not profit, $(-)$
    but righteousness saves from death. $(+)$
The Lord will not let the righteous go hungry, $(+)$
    but he thwarts the craving of the wicked. $(-)$
A lazy hand causes poverty, $(-)$
    but the hand of the diligent makes rich. $(+)$

These verses all conform to Menachem ha-Meiri's first principle, consisting of verses having two opposing values. However, these are not binary propositions such as the quadripartites studied above, not statements of evaluation but rather of assertion or valuation, stating what is viewed as positive or praiseworthy and what is negative or blameworthy. What seems noteworthy, rather, is the chiastic structure according to which values are presented, suggesting a pattern of organization that goes beyond individual verses and which is based, once again, on a rhythmical presentation of value-statements. The suggestion here would seem to be that vv. 1–2 (and also 3–4), chiastically joined, be considered together for purposes of interpretation.

Patterns other than chiasmus are frequent, suggesting that Menachem ha-Meiri's principle 1 can be further refined. Consider the next four verses in Prov 10 (5–8):

A son who gathers in summer is prudent, $(+)$
    but a son who sleeps in harvest brings shame. $(-)$
Blessings are upon the head of the righteous, $(+)$
    but violence covers the mouth of the wicked. $(-)$
The memory of the righteous is a blessing, $(+)$
    but the fame of the wicked will rot. $(-)$
The wise of heart will accept commandments, $(+)$
    but one of foolish lips will come to ruin. $(-)$

Here we have the same verse composition consisting of one plus and one minus value, and again the group of four follows a consistent pattern. Here, however, all verses proceed from $(+)$ to $(-)$ (cf. also 10:27–11:2, where there is a sequence of eight such verses).

Again, the purpose of this is merely to show the importance of value in such proverb or wisdom collections, to the degree that values seem to have become the basis of organization of patterns of verses in their succession. From the above it seems that things have (positive or negative) value both in themselves and in relation, here viewed as particular *sequences of value-*

statements. I also suggest that such sequences have not only organizational but interpretative importance, as statements of the purposeful direction of values. Consider the following: "Don't love as one who is going to hate, but hate as one who is going to love" (Aristotle, *Rhet.* 2.21 [cf. Russo 1983, 124–25]). Here we have the familiar paradox of a hatred (that leads to and thus perhaps also arises from love) that is *better than* love (if it leads to hatred). This saying paradigmatically states the point of Koh 3:2–8, according to which $(-+)$ is better than or a potent wisdom alternative to $(+-)$.

(C) RELATIVE VALUE

We are distrustful of formulas, perhaps because they imply rigidity of thinking and judgment. It is therefore important to inspect a bit further the flexibility of the formulas themselves. Consider the following variant of the better-than structure: "It is easier to remove a happy man from his happiness than a sad man from his sadness" (*MF:*19, no. 40). This is actually a better-than structure in which the third member is stated before the second. Thus:

1. happy man and happiness $(++)$
2. sad man and removed sadness $(-+)$
3. happy man and removed happiness $(+-)$
4. sad man and sadness $(--)$

This rather technical formulation does not seem to make much sense. The meaning, however, is that between the happy and the sad person there is the person who is neither, but this actually implies two possible situations, one of which is definitely preferable to the other: a sad man who is cured, and a happy man who no longer is happy. The wisdom writer thus suggests that the mean between happiness and sadness is actually twofold, depending on the previous state (or, again, as in our analysis of Koh 3:2–8, the direction in which one is moving), and thus easier to reach from one direction than from the other. Or, more statically viewed, the absence of sadness is better than the absence of happiness.

The wisdom meaning of such sayings can be further analyzed by considering another formal variant of better-than that states the *best* and *worst* or the two extremes: "The best of the good is to do it; the worst of the the bad is to do it" (*MF:*18, no. 20). This can be restated theoretically as follows:

1. good and doing it $(++)$
2. bad and not doing it $(-+)$
3. good and not doing it $(+-)$
4. bad and doing it $(--)$

Note that in this example the predicate or second topic changes value according to the value of the first topic, suggesting that in substance this saying is possessive rather than conjunctive. The superlatives of good and bad require their being placed in propositions 1 and 4, since the precise meaning of these positions is "best" and "worst." The better-than statement again presents the exception of "when is the bad preferable to the good?" The meaning, far from trite or purely logical, involves one of the deepest paradoxes of wisdom literature: "The bad which does not come into being is better than the good which does not come into being" (*MF:*5, line 6). Of the several forms of restating this, I propose the following one:

1. the good man who exists $(++)$:   is "good"
2. the bad man who doesn't exist $(-+)$:   is "not bad"
3. the good man who doesn't exist $(+-)$:   is "not good"
4. the bad man who exists $(--)$:   is "bad"

Thus, the abstract structure generates a graded series of valuations, none of which is identical with any other. It seems preferable to consider existence or nonexistence as attributes of the basic topic and the variants of good and bad as commentary. This nonexistence may be conceived as the prevention of existence, as I do here, or, alternately, as the termination of existence, as in La Rochefoucauld's maxim:

La fin du bien est un mal; la fin du mal est un bien.

The termination of good is an evil; the termination of evil is a good.
(1976, 149)

This maxim was not printed in standard editions of the *Maximes,* undoubtedly because, as Madame de Sablé complained (La Rochefoucauld 1976, 295), it was unclear or, more likely, too paradoxical. At any rate, the maxim forms propositions 3 and 2, respectively, of the quadripartite.

Santob de Carrión's version of this thought is particularly dramatic: "It is certainly worse for one wicked man to rise up among the people than for ten righteous men to perish" (Santob, lines 1105–08). Again, this text is of the possessive class. Examples abound: "The death of honorable men is better than the rule of the lowly" (*MF:*42, no. 4; also *Bocados de oro* 1879, 264).[17]

A further example of best and worst will help clarify this relation of topics, as well as the relative status of values: "Wealth is good if without sin; poverty is evil if resulting from sin" (Sirach 13:24).[18] Here is the structural restatement:

1. wealth and sinless
4. poverty and sinful

To read this as a causative, as Segal proposes (1964, 86), implies an interesting causative also in the first statement: one is wealthy because of sinlessness. The main point I wish to clarify, however, is the implied intermediate statements:

2. poverty and sinless
3. wealth and sinful

What the full structural restatement help us understand is less the superiority of sinlessness over its opposite (this is, after all, a **W**isdom given) or even that the topics "wealth and poverty" are morally neutral. The point, rather, is that these topics have value: poverty is negative and wealth is positive *from a wisdom as well as a worldly perspective.* Or, at the very least, wealth cannot be considered a priori as a negative value.

(D) CAUSE AND RESULT PROVERBS

Cause and result structures, also known as act/consequence relationships, are a most common type in wisdom texts, perhaps because the chief intent of such traditional sources as the Book of Proverbs is to warn how certain results follow from certain actions.[19] Indeed, one of the basic doctrines of all

17. The avoidance of evil, whether moral fault or physical harm, is constantly stressed in wisdom texts; e.g. Prov 16:17: "The highway of the upright departs from evil; one who would preserve his life watches his way."

18. RSV: "Riches are good if they are free from sin, and poverty is evil in the opinion of the ungodly."

19. In the discussion of logical connectives in such sayings as Prov 11:2 ("When pride comes, then comes disgrace") the terms *cause* and *result* are here preferred to "act/consequence" terminology, which seems inappropriate even to designate sayings of heavy moral import such as "Out of the wicked comes forth wickedness" (1 Sam 24:14 E13) because such causes designate not acts but rather dispositions or kinds of person.

wisdom literature is that of reward and punishment, the belief that our well-being is related to our behavior.[20] This notion is of course not restricted to wisdom literature, and even within this camp there were discordant voices. One strain of thinking in Kohelet rejects it outright, and Job, while not calling into question the principle itself, denies that it is justly applied to his own case. In the view of the Book of Jonah, the ultimate guarantor of this doctrine, God Himself, is also viewed as its subverter, since He is willing to let off the wicked of Nineveh scotfree. As the Jerusalem Talmud movingly put it, distinguishing wisdom's (and prophesy's) approach from God's own:

> They asked of wisdom: "What is the sinner's punishment?" Wisdom replied: "Misfortune pursues sinners" (Prov 13:21). They asked prophesy: "What is the sinner's punishment?" Prophesy replied: "The soul that sins shall die" (Ezek 18:4). They asked of God: "What is the sinner's punishment?" God replied: "Let him repent and he will be forgiven." (Jerusalem Talmud, Makkot, Halakah 2:6)

Westermann (1971) has argued that act/consequence is indeed the essential message of wisdom literature in general, and even this text can be viewed not as subverting the generally accepted view but rather as confirming it, since God's grace is conditional (on repentance). Honein's formulation is axiomatic:

> No good deed without its reward; no bad deed without its punishment. (*BP*: line 32)

> He who does good finds good; he who does evil finds evil. (*BP*: line 44)

> Righteousness leads to life and he who pursues evil is headed for death. (Prov 11:19)

Such claims are not always advanced in any absolute sense, and this may be why the form of such sayings is often less assertive than the above examples.[21] Indeed, although such cause and result statements can be considered as the soul of the didactic function of proverbs, such designs are not always apparent from external form. For example, causal structures are typically *equational,* thus revealing an affinity with that type. Consider the synonymy in the

20. The connection between cause and result is always implicit and is often clearly stated; see, for example, Prov 26:27; Koh 10:8; Sirach 27:27; Ps 7:16–17 E15–16; BT Sotah 7a: "According to the measure that a man measures, it shall be measured to him."

21. For example, simple juxtaposition of cause and result is used instead of assertion (see Williams 1981, 18–20).

following: "A wise son makes a glad father; a foolish son *is* a sorrow to his mother" (Prov 10:1). Others take on a *conjunctive* form, such as Dundes's well-known example (1981, 55): "you can't have your cake *and* eat it too," which implies two complementary propositions:

1. eat and don't have $(+-)$
2. don't eat and have $(-+)$

These in turn become propositions in complementary distribution, excluding the propositions "you can't eat and have" $(++)$ and also "you can't not eat and not have" $(--)$. But this example is conjunctive only in appearance; its real structure of *implication* is rather close to the equational and in fact can be stated in that form:

1. eating = not having $(+ = -)$
2. not eating = having $(- = +)$

This is, of course, not purely equational, since we have seen that in these structures of experience pure equations do not exist, but in order to generate the other two statements of the quadripartite a semantic change would have to occur, such as changing the meaning of "having" from "having in one's possession" to "having as a part of one's body." Thus,

3. eating = having $(++)$
4. not eating = not having $(--)$

It will be noticed that both examples are stated as observations, leading perhaps to a fundamental distinction between result proverbs of *observation* (recording the "ways of the world") and result proverbs of *condition* (stating the results that will follow *if...*). In both cases, however, as opposed to other proverbial genres such as the maxim, which is expressed in an eternal present tense, wisdom proverbs typically look to the future in the form of prediction of certain results from certain causes.[22] The first observes with disapproval the way things actually happen and implies ways of evaluating certain situations and persons. For example, "Ganders eating up rice plants: the one who is stealing from his neighbor cries the loudest" (Andriantsilaniarivo 1982, 274–75). Such observations, often based on paradox and full of irony,

22. In Chapter 4.1 below, the Anchos story alerts us to the status of wisdom proverbs as a weakened form of prophecy.

offer advice and caution as well: Be on guard against such people! By a contrast that is more stylistic than substantial, a proverb such as "haste makes waste" is not only an observation and a caution but an implied condition as well; it is in fact more the latter because it both offers concrete advice and is turned toward the future: if you make haste you will suffer loss.

(E) BEYOND COMPARE: THE VALUE OF WISDOM

What wisdom writers sought to do was make relative judgments, evaluations comparing the less with the more through such devices as "better-than." Some think that this method is opposed to the absolutism of priestly and prophetic literature. Perhaps, but the point is not that wisdom is relative but that the world and especially language are, and the tools or methods must be appropriate to the task. To observe that wisdom can be applied relatively and to things indifferent—what is here referred to as the "ways of the world"—is not the same as saying that it is relative by its very nature. If this were the case, then passages like "The Lord by wisdom founded the earth . . . " (Prov 3:19–20) would be incomprehensible.

To recall the discussion of better-than proverbs above, it was seen how the first or **w**orldly topic of proposition 3 is normally considered superior to the first or **w**orldly topic of 2, but this is the case because in such propositions the latter becomes qualified so radically by the **W**isdom topic of 2 as to be considered inferior. The crucial term of such structures, the one upon which the value of the entire proverb depends, therefore, is the **W**isdom topic of proposition 2. Consider the following: "The hatred of a sage is better than the love of a fool" (*MF:* 49, line 34; also Merkle 1921, 29). Thus,

2. hatred *of a sage* $(-+)$
3. love of a fool $(+-)$

Here it is asserted that even the *hatred* of a sage is "better than" even the *beneficence* of a fool because the sage is really beyond comparison with the fool, of a totally different substance or nature. In a similar manner, the mere tail of a lion is "better than" even the head of a mere fox, again because of the incomparable superiority of the lion. The point was belabored by sages and collectors; Santob de Carrión, for example:

Quien peso de un dinero	He who has a coin's weight
Ha mas de entendimiento,	more of intellect,
Por aquello señero	through this alone he is
Vale un omre por çiento.	worth a hundred others.
(Santob, lines 1917–20)	

In this regard no text is more eloquent that Prov 8:11, where the second clause of the parallelistic line indeed reinforces the first, but does so by negating the comparison:[23] "For wisdom is better than jewels, and all that you may desire *cannot compare* with her"[24] (Prov 8:11 [RSV]). In other words, a strong reading of this text yields the point of view that "no-thing in this world can be compared to wisdom." Finally, commenting on the comparison of wisdom to riches in Prov 3:14, Menachem ha-Meiri (1969) in fact asserts that "there is no comparison between the two." The typical form of denying the common ground between the two is, thus, to deny the comparison by using one term as a figure, on the model of the Rabbinic tag "what is poverty? Poverty of knowledge." In other words, the only "poverty" worthy of discussion is ignorance.

An interesting variant of this approach can be seen in what may be called the Excluded Three or, formulaicly, *one that is not four.* For example, in Prov 3:17, Wisdom is compared to a road: "Its highways are ways of pleasantness and all of its paths are peace." This suggests the following restatement in the form of a commentary:

1. paths are pleasant but not safe $(+-)$
2. highways are not pleasant but safe $(-+)$
3.
4. wisdom is both pleasant and safe $(++)$

This commentary, added by Menachem ha-Meiri's scribe (1969, 36), has an interesting parallel in *MF:* 20, no. 49: "Do not choose short paths [i.e., paths, even if they are short]; rather choose highways even though they are long." In our example the third proposition is not given because it is of no interest; one assumes that it is the total absence of any kind of path, as walking through thick woods, for example.

Thus, from a strictly wisdom perspective, whatever does not measure up to the "best" is of no value or interest whatever. Here are further examples:

23. See Chapter 2.4, "Proverbs of Simple Preference."

24. The final clause may literally be rendered as follows: "and no things can compare with it." Cf. also 8:19: "My fruit is better than gold, even fine gold, and my yield than choice silver."

There are four kinds of words. Those that

1. benefit one person and harm another $(+-)$
2. benefit neither speaker nor hearer (idle words) $(--)$
3. offer no benefit to speaker and harm to another (slander) $(--)$
4. benefit both speaker and hearer (words of wisdom) $(++)$

Menachem ha-Meiri (1969, 96)[25]

The following example occurs as a warning to avoid vain actions (Menachem ha-Meiri 1969, 159):

There are four kinds of actions. Those that have

1. no intention [and no result] $(--)$
2. a bad intention [and ?] $(-?)$
3. a good intention but no result $(+-)$
4. a good intention and a good result $(++)$

As opposed to the better-than pattern that establishes gradations and, for that reason, focuses on the intermediate propositions 2 and 3 and, indeed, could even leave out the extremities 1 and 4, these latter patterns focus only on "what is the best" and can thus exclude or neglect the other three propositions. This pattern typically groups the three lesser categories and has no interest in distinguishing, for example, the "not good" and the "bad," except in that they are both opposed to "the good" and thus both $(-)$. Thus, among conjunctive statements the better-than variety, in its typical desire to establish gradations, results in a balanced structure, whereas the "best of all" variety is often imbalanced. The two approaches recall the two Stoic levels of wisdom: the graded kind for learners, and the all-or-nothing kind for the true sage.

---

25. See also Abot 2:1: "Rabbi [Judah the Prince] said: 'What is the straight path that a person should choose: one that is good both for him and for his fellow.'"

4

THE SAGES' MESSAGE

1. A Parable of Wisdom's Origins: The Cranes of Ibycus

Historical and chronological attempts to solve the puzzle of the origin of proverbs usually flounder hopelessly in the fog of prehistory, oral transmission, and folkloric anonymity. No less frustrating is the question of definitions, for, despite the recent increase in paremiology or proverb research, definitions typically take comfort in Archer Taylor's (1931) declaration—with which I strongly disagree—that proverbs are known by their undefinable quality. The questions of origin and definition may be related, as in the now popular characterization of proverbs as "the wisdom of many and the wit of one" (Taylor 1931, 3; cf. Mieder and Dundes 1981, 3–9). The cleverness of this formula is that it acknowledges two circumstantial probabilities: that a proverb was originally spoken by one specific (though usually anonymous) speaker at a precise (though usually unknown) moment in time, and that it "belongs" to many because the original speaker either gleaned its message from many people or merely expressed what everyone really knew.

Wisdom literature, from its inception and well into modern times, is at variance with this view. It argues that it is wisdom itself, rather than its mere expression, that issues from a single individual, the sage, who quarries it from both the rough granite of personal experience and the depths of his own knowledge rather than from any consensus—indeed, wisdom is most often a resolute *challenge* to consensus; and it is often the many who, through successive elaborations, confer its final, witty form. From a wisdom perspective the current catchphrase can thus be turned on its head: Proverbs are the wisdom of one and the wit of many.

What then are proverbs, and where do they come from? Consonant with my approach to structure through traditional texts, I again revert to the ongoing wisdom tradition itself and seek clues from its own self-understanding. One answer, taken from a major collection of wisdom literature, Honein Ibn Isaac's ninth-century proverb compilation,[1] deals with origins and definitions through parable and even in the form of a puzzle. To understand this approach one needs to consider the literary context of wisdom collections, that is to say, to view the collection itself as a context and to begin to reflect on the nature of wisdom collections and anthologies (we have few generic studies of these minor genres). What is initially most striking about the collections is their heterogeneity, their kaleidoscopic variety, the apparent unconnectedness of their elements, their haiku or fragmentary nature. The outstanding exception of the extended narration of Prov 1–9 cannot be adequately explained by assuming different historical origins, for one still must explain its literary purpose, that is, why a later editor used it as a preface to such a collection. Here I propose to study an analogous case, in which a lengthy collection of proverbs is paradoxically introduced by a most unproverbial sequence.

From a literary point of view, the "Book of Good Proverbs" of Honein Ibn Isaac is prefaced by a frame-narrative. What is initially interesting for our purposes is the wisdom ambiance of the story: the hero is a sage and the climax occurs during a wisdom festival. By the end of the tale, however, one can see beyond the trappings; the story of Anchos becomes a dress rehearsal, I propose, of the wisdom enterprise itself. Here is the text of the frame-narrative:

The Story of Anchos [Ibycus] the Poet[2]

There was a King in Greece, Comedes by name, who wrote to Anchos the Poet, inviting him to come to him with all his wisdom.

---

1. See above, Introduction 4.
2. Anchos is his name in the Spanish version; in the Hebrew he is called Inkas. The reference,

He packed up his books and his money and set out. And as he passed through a deserted area, worthless thieves fell upon him, intending to kill him and take his money. And he forswore them by God almighty (may He be blessed!) that they should desist, taking his money and allowing him to continue his way, but they refused and gathered to kill him. And he glanced to the right and the left, looking for help. And when he saw that there was none to be found, he raised his eyes to heaven and saw cranes flying in the sky. And, seeing that no other help was forthcoming, he shouted to the flying cranes: "I have found no one to help me and no one to see me. *Be the witnesses and avengers of my blood.*" But the scoffers made fun and said one to another: "This man has no sense, and *he who has no sense, there is no sin in killing.*" Whereupon they murdered him and divided up his money and clothes and returned to their hiding place.

When word of Anchos's death reached the people of his city, they searched for the murderers but were unsuccessful, until the Greeks' great Festival day arrived. They gathered in the city of Anchos the Poet in their places of meeting to hear words of wisdom and philosophy. And people came from everywhere, to be seen and to gather together, and it was their custom to read from their books of wisdom on that day. And the murderers of Anchos the Poet also came and mixed with the crowd. And while they were there a crane flew over them and screeched. And they said one to another: "Behold the avengers of the blood of Anchos the Fool!" But one of the citizens next to them overheard their words and relayed them to the King. And they took them and forced them to confess and claimed his money from them, and they died the same death. And the crane did indeed avenge his death: Know and reflect that *the Avenger is in the heavens!*

This tale, of course, is the famous "Cranes of Ibycus," purporting to recount the death of the Greek lyric poet who flourished in the sixth century B.C.E.[3] The puzzle of the connection between this tale and the long lists of wisdom sayings that follow cannot be satisfactorily resolved by the mere observation that Anchos was a sage and they too were spoken by sages. The

---

of course, is to Ibycus, and the corruption of *b* by *n* is easily explained as due to a misplaced dot in the Arabic original. Similarly, the initial *A* of Anchos is due to the absence of vocalization in the Arabic.

3. It is listed in Stith Thompson (1955–58, no. N271.3). The story has had wide diffusion in both popular and literary circles (Amalfi 1896; Bolte and Polivka 1963, 2:532) and is the subject of Schiller's well-known ballad "Die Kraniche des Ibykus."

problem can be focused, rather, by the literary consideration that the tale of Anchos here serves as a frame-story for the entire collection.[4] The introductory story becomes especially crucial in the absence of an ongoing subplot, since it must assume the burden of presenting the entire book and, possibly, suggesting a unifying theme or pattern. Why, then, was the tale of Anchos added to the collection, and in the opening position? Does it have merely aesthetic value, or, as I argue, does it constitute a warning and, indeed, even a paradigmatic proverb in its own right?[5]

At least two of Honein's possible Greek sources are known: Antipater of Sidon, the Greek epigrammatist who wrote around 130 B.C.E., and Plutarch (*Moralia,* "De Garrulitate," 1970, 439), whose version is well worth quoting:

> [Ibycus's murderers] were sitting in a theater, and when cranes came in sight, they laughed and whispered to each other that the avengers of Ibycus were come. Persons sitting near overheard them, and since Ibycus had disappeared and a long time had been sought, they caught at his remark and reported it to the magistrate. . . . They were not punished by the cranes but compelled to confess the murder by the infirmity of their own tongues, as if it were some Fury or spirit of vengeance.

Such an interpretation indeed constitutes a warning, but against garrulousness and directed to thieves and murderers! However, Plutarch does give the folk motif a decidedly moral orientation, setting it off from similar tales about the "avenging sun" and, indeed, from those versions in which it is the birds themselves which follow the murderers and point them out—traces of this ancient theme survive in Grimm's Tale 115, "Die klare Sonne bringt's an den

4. It is well known that frame-stories play an important role in medieval *exempla* anthologies. In Boccaccio the frame furnishes a subplot that sustains its own interest and also unifies the collection by providing an ongoing commentary. A key moment in such narratives is the opening one, since it must set the tone for the entire collection. In a work to which we have referred constantly and that contains one of the major proverb collections of the Middle Ages, Juan Manuel's *El conde Lucanor,* the frame-story provides an "atmosphere," indeed, "an introduction and a justification for the entire collection" (Sturm 1969, 286–87).

5. It is important to notice the different focus of the titles of our book. The one in the partial Arabic version in the Oxford MS is the most restrictive: *Idjtima'at al-falasifah,* "meetings of the sages," referring only to the first main section, or to roughly one-fifth of the total Spanish text. The Spanish "buenos proverbios" is more extensive; it regards the first two sections as paramount, consisting of pearls of proverbial wisdom-sayings strung together without apparent concern for their order and each valuable in its own right. Al-Harizi's title "Teachings or Warnings" (*MF*) is even more comprehensive, since it would include the narrative portions as well: the tale of Aristotle's rise to fame (9–10), and the legends surrounding Alexander at the end. According to this view, all aspects, the narratives as well as the sayings, form part of the sages' warnings and chastisements.

Tag."[6] Plutarch removes any trace of such magic and confines his explanation to human psychology, thus marking an important distinction separating
all the versions of our tale into two camps (Köhler 1900, 2:563–64).

One element of the story certainly appealed to our author's aesthetic and
didactic sense, the public wisdom-setting of the discovery of the murderers.
He never tires of mentioning the ceremony, the trappings of splendor, the
regal attire of the sages, especially "when they gathered together in their
schools during their festivals" (4, also 8–9). Such opulence forms the invari-
able (courtly and school) setting for these feasts of knowledge, attended by
the pomp of royalty, and this initial scene is a model for later such gatherings.
If Honein knew Plutarch's version, then his change of location from the
theater to the assembly of sages is self-serving in two ways: it reinforces
wisdom's prestige and anticipates the first major section of the book. It raises
a problem, however; while one can imagine the murderers at the theater,
such "worthless fellows" (*bnei belia'l*) surely had no interest in learning
wisdom, which took place, according to the Spanish, in an *yglesia* or church!
Our texts seem to have anticipated this objection, for the Spanish text
proposes that "all the people" attended such events (2), and the Hebrew
version mischievously suggests that they came "to be seen" (*le-hera'ot*). This
detail balances the author's uncritical enthusiasm for such ceremonies with a
touch of irony, by intimating that mere attendance at lectures is no guarantee
that one will pass the course.

A second reason for including the frame-tale at the head of the collection
has to do with its religious character; one of its messages is that God is to be
feared (Prov 14:26). When Honein draws the moral of his story at the end,
this is in fact the only message that he stresses: "[God] hears those who call
upon Him with good will and a sincere heart." Since such collections speak
very little about God, it was therefore felt all the more urgent to begin the
book with this theme, whereupon the author could pass on to the matters at
hand. Moderns are apt to regard such evidence as proof that the author was
not really religious, but this seems to me to be misconstruing the evidence.[7]
In the *Libro de los buenos proverbios* the initial message of reward and especially
punishment is that all actions have their consequences, and that even when
the doer cares little for his own opinion or that of his fellow, he still should

6. See Bolte and Polivka (1963, ad. loc.); see also the interesting midrash quoted by Rashi in his
comment on Num 25:4.

7. An analogous case is Santob de Carrión, who also avoids explicit theologizing but prefaces his
Proverbios morales with an account of personal repentance and the necessity of return to God (see Perry
1987b).

fear God. There is also the likelihood that the author gave stylistic importance to the injunction of Prov 1:7, that fear of the Lord is the beginning of
wisdom, that is, of wisdom and also of wisdom's discourses. This also
explains, as the author remarks, why the sages prayed before expounding
their views (9).

A third issue, in a book dedicated entirely to words of the sages, addresses
the value of such words. Were the thieves correct in their epithet "Anchos the
fool"? Their downfall is an object-lesson, pointing to the necessity of listening and reflecting carefully upon the words of the sages (Prov 13:14). This is
in perfect conformity with the total aim of the book, which is to praise the
sages and preserve their wisdom.

In addition to such warnings, I would like to propose—and this is my
main point—that this story provides an example, indeed a paradigm,
for the creation of proverbs and wisdom sayings. From this point of view,
the central theme of the story is not the rich assemblies of the sages
or God's justice or the punishment of the wicked but the kernel of wisdom
uttered by the main protagonist, which then becomes the central agent
of the tale, challenging the thieves and the author for an interpretation and
bringing about the resolution of the plot. This would be an example of a
story in which the plot hinges on a wisdom saying (Hasan-Rokem 1983),
where, in fact, it is not the protagonists that are the characters but their
sayings.

According to our tale the wisdom saying arises according to precise steps
and with the following characteristics:

1. The saying arises from a sage's experience, in this case the rather
harrowing experience of being robbed and facing imminent death.

2. The sage expresses the first but stylistically not the final version of
the saying. He looks up toward the birds and says: "Be the witnesses and
avengers of my blood." At this stage, in fact, his wise words are not meant
as a proverb and do not constitute a wisdom "saying"; this more-or-less
literary transformation will be done later. His words are rather to be considered as a wise action subject (as are all of a sage's actions) to study and
interpretation.

3. The first stage of the words' interpretation and constitution as a wisdom
saying occurs immediately; the thieves interpret these words as a false saying
and, in a lapidary style intended to mock the sage's so-called wisdom, retort
with their own "countersaying": "He who has no sense, there is no sin in
killing."[8]

8. The Spanish particularizes the saying and therefore loses the ironical repartee: "Such a stupid

4. The thieves misinterpret the words a second time, at the festival, when they repeat them in a mocking tone. The point seems to be their inability to interpret wisdom correctly.

5. In the Hebrew version the tale has a summarizing apothegm:[9] "The Searcher is in the heavens," and it is preceded by a formulaic wisdom warning: "Know and reflect that . . . " This concluding proverb constitutes a later, literary version of Anchos's saying. It is important to note that this final version does not occur in the narrative itself; rather, it is an interpretative act formulated by the narrator, Honein.

The introductory narrative has thus represented the first stage in the life of a wisdom saying, from the moment of its utterance by a sage and through its interpretations and misinterpretations until it finds its place, as it were, in a collection of this kind. The placement of the Anchos tale in the opening position carries the clear suggestion that all such sayings have like origins and deserve equal consideration. Honein's introductory tale thus combines aesthetic appeal and didactic utility with yet a third feature, one that critics recognize in many works of literature: a theory of its own writing and reading. Through the tale of Ibycus, Honein was able to portray what his sumptuous feasts of knowledge merely glorified: the life-cycle of wisdom sayings in a real-life context. The tale exemplifies the book's content; it represents, performatively more than analytically, a theory of the origin and nature of wisdom sayings.

(A) THE WISDOM OF ONE

The Anchos story furnishes a practical definition of wisdom proverbs in its suggestion that such sayings have their origin in a sage. That is to say, not only does the sage speak wisdom or act wisely but also, more to the point, wisdom is what the sage speaks or does; his actions and words are always wise and are, in fact, definitive of wisdom itself: "Wisdom is the fruit of the sages and the harvest of the wise" (*MF*: 7, no. 4).[10] In Jewish tradition the thought acquired proverbial status: "Even the secular conversation of the sages requires

---

person there is no sin in killing." Incidentally, the words were interpreted by the thieves very much to the disadvantage of Ibycus, who either did not properly gauge their reaction or, perhaps, had judged the case to be already desperate.

9. Juan Manuel works in exactly the same way in his *El conde Lucanor*: first he narrates a traditional tale and then summarizes it sententiously in his own words (cf. Perry 1987a).

10. "La sapiençia es renta de los sabios e argumento dellos" (*BP*:8).

study" (BT ʿAboda Zara 19b). In its origins, therefore, Wisdom is *the wisdom of one*.

This idea is a common assumption of wisdom texts and should be considered in the context of the frequent authorial superscription of traditional collections. In the biblical Book of Proverbs, for example, the subject is announced as "the sayings *of the sages* and *their* riddles" (1:6) and in the original Hebrew the title of the book is in the construct state, again stressing that these are proverbs "of Solomon." Likewise, the title of the Book of Ecclesiastes may focus not on a collection of sayings but rather on their sayer: Kohelet, "the Collector."[11] It is true that the assertion of personal authorship—whether true or fictitious—gradually yielded to the convention of anonymity as such sayings were copied and transferred to other anthologies (see Walsh 1976, 378). This phenomenon seems due either to the loss of correct traditions or, more probably and significantly, to the disappearance of live sages from the social scene, thus reducing such attributions to mere appeals to authority but devoid of any real-life significance. The consequences of such a state of affairs, from a wisdom perspective, can be weighed from the optimistic opposing point of view: "He who cites a saying in the name of its original sayer brings salvation to the world" (BT Hullin 104a). Jaded modern readers may, of course, prefer the more skeptical (and later) view that such attributions of personal origin were mere enhancements of authority. It seems possible, however, that the intent was just the opposite. Since it is clear that the normal performance of proverbs is citational by nature, a rhetorical trick to line up the anonymous and thus more imposing wisdom of the ages behind one's point of view, the attribution to a single source or sayer can be seen as a principled refusal to resort to such tactics (Grésillon and Maingueneau 1989, 111–13).

Wisdom is thus the "wisdom of one" because it originates from a single source. Such a perspective dispels a sense of abstraction and diffusiveness often associated with such sayings, by stressing that wisdom does not come from either some otherworldly source or anonymous group but rather from a specific and unique person. This is not to deny that, as the Book of Proverbs also insists, its sayings are the forms of wisdom and not only of wisdom writers, and that it is its discovery and initial articulation that is granted to individuals who are wise. In my usage, therefore, "saying" is an

---

11. This plausible hypothesis has been stated by Crenshaw (1987, 33), who declares that if the name "could also apply to a gathering of objects, then Qohelet might be a 'collector of proverbs,' as the epilogist remembers his teacher" (12:9–11).

inclusive and neutral indication, allowing a broad range of literary forms (proverbs, aphorisms, riddles, and the like), but in a wisdom context it is always referred to a qualified "sayer." The most pertinent definition of such utterances is therefore *words said by a sage.*[12]

By a sage (or sages) and not by the many: here it is necessary to return to our opening distinction between "popular" and learned sayings, that is, those that push propaganda versus those that set out to provoke thought. A sage has an awareness that is often communicated only through paradox, something that jars our "normal" consciousness and values because of its dissonance. To say to a hungry person that "there is no bread without Torah" (Abot 3:17) is perhaps to go against the evidence of daily experience. It is surely to lead that person in a circuitous direction, and to call such wise advice practical seems to me a strain on normal usage. Surely it addresses practical matters (hunger, power, etc.), but not in its own terms, and one would be hard put to speak of a consensus here (except, perhaps, "in the long run").

Behind the one (the sage) there is of course the One (God), and one senses that this dimension is often assumed, though rarely mentioned. In Honein's reading of the folkloric tale of Anchos, the birds acquire a new interpretive dimension. They symbolize not only the nagging of conscience, as Plutarch insisted, but also the justice of God above the heads of the murderers. Or, perhaps, the birds picture the very words of the sage, as Honein seems to suggest in a striking comparison: "Our hearts are bound by the cables of their sayings, and these sayings exist [in us] like the existence of the soul in the air."[13] The birds both come from above and are responsive to Anchos, just as wise sayings come both from the sayer but also from Wisdom.

(B) THE WIT OF MANY

What then is the message of transmission and of the collections that often sponsor them? I would stress that this indicates a joining of the collective and the individual voice. The speaker is part of a tradition, a transmitter, an authorized interpreter, and to preface a saying by such a formula as "Joshua the son of X says" is to include the latter in that tradition. On the one hand, he is only an individual and his words can be criticized on that basis. On the other, his words are quoted, transmitted, learned, transferred to different life

12. The opposite view, according to which proverbs never have individual origins and are statements that anyone could have made, is expressed by Whiting (1931, 48).

13. Only in the Hebrew text: "U-bahem qiyyumam ke-qiyyum ha-nepesh ba-'awir," *MF* 4.

contexts, so that the result is the saying of sages (in the plural). It is in fact pluralization at this level that forms the basis of what is called the wisdom enterprise.[14]

At times this inclusion is more aggressive and active, and again it is Kohelet that sets the rule that tests the standard: "Kohelet was not only himself a sage but also added to wisdom by teaching the people knowledge. He listened and pondered, righting [*tikken*] many proverbs" (Koh 12:9).[15] The suggestion is that collectors not only quote and preserve through writing but also compose and even adapt and correct through "righting."

Other models exist for the passage from the one to the many, from what may be regarded as a wisdom challenge to a (successful) interpretation or commentary. Consider Samson's provocative riddle to the Philistines:[16]

> Out of the eater came something to eat.
> Out of the strong came something sweet.
> (Judg 14:14)

Here the challenge is to interpret the sage's "raw experience," so to speak (14: 8–9), and the solution is pluralized in its presentation by the "men of the city":

> What is sweeter than honey?
> What is stronger than a lion?
> (Judg 14:18)

Here the right answer was punished, rather than rewarded, because it was derived not through thinking but rather trickery. Similarly, Anchos's murderers were also punished, because they came up with the wrong answer and were thus guilty of *wrong* thinking.

---

14. There is an interesting variant of this process in recent criticism, in the attempt to include such biblical books as the Song of Songs, Ruth, and Esther in the wisdom canon on the pretext that they are "within the purview of the sages' goals" (Murphy 1981, xiii).

15. The translation is mine; see my forthcoming commentary (Perry 1993). For the pun "righting" RSV has "arranging" and Gordis (1968), "fashioning," closer to the sense that Kohelet was not only a collector of the work of others but wrote his own compositions. I suggest that there is an additional sense here, an even more active participation, since Kohelet actually corrected or "made straight" (cf. Koh 7:13) other sayings, perhaps by glosses, that then became part of the older sayings.

16. I am grateful to David Jobling (private communication) for this example.

2. Didacticism

Thus far the Anchos tale has told us a great deal about wisdom sayings, what we may call their single origin or first stage. The second stage in the life of such sayings deals with their workings once they have been created and go on their way to further reinterpretation and collection by the many. In the Spanish version Anchos is called both a "profeta" and a "versificador." The Hebrew retains the second epithet but omits the first, undoubtedly because this would cause confusion in the minds of Jews, for whom there was no possible comparison between such "wisdom," made up of human opinions, and the authentic tradition of the prophets of the Bible (see Menachem ha-Meiri, 1969, introduction). However, the epithet does refer to a most important aspect of wisdom teaching. Just as a prophet's message always joins two time dimensions, the present and the future, in moral proverbs the "saying" intervenes at two (Menachem ha-Meiri 1969, 51) crucial stages in the teaching process: before the act and after the act. The first is perhaps the more important, since it can help avert an evil deed in the form of a warning of the evil results that will follow from a given wicked action. In other words, a saying presents a prediction; it is a concrete application of a universal principle and thus constitutes a weakened form of prophesy.

The second phase of the application of the saying is often neglected but is no less crucial to the workings of the proverb's teaching power. This occurs *after* the evil action has been performed and the evil consequences have happened. At this juncture the saying returns in the form "I told you so," or, to use the expression from a tradition that is perhaps related, "a little birdie told me" (Koh 10:20). Jolles's complaint that proverbs do not prophesy: "In proverbs the well is covered up only after the child has drowned" (1958, 158–59) is at least an acknowledgment that they can exercise this judgmental function.

Finally, the sage is also called a versifier. Is this a requirement? And are all versifiers ipso facto sages? The meaning seems to be a rather simple one. In the words of an anonymous fifteenth-century glosser of such sayings, "these verses are most notable writings which all men should memorize, for rhymed writings are more easily memorized than prose" (cited in Perry 1987b, 174). Wisdom sayings must be versified, epigrammatic, because they should be memorized. Why? Because, at crucial moments of acting and evaluating our actions, the sayings of the sages stand as prophets and as witnesses and must rise up in the "heavens" of the intellect and memory to warn or to judge, like the cranes of Ibycus.

The first aspect is commonly acknowledged (Crenshaw 1981, 17). Wisdom seeks to shape present or future actions and attitudes, through advice on what to pursue and warning on what to avoid. The second promotes reflection on *past* experience and events. The connection between the two is more intimate, however; generally speaking, even when wisdom is simple good advice of a practical (and not necessarily moral) nature (Crenshaw 1981, 16f.), it always implies value judgments on the whole of life and sees all time dimensions as geared to final ends.

Another way to review the didactic component is through the notion of persuasion or authority. Why do speakers choose to interrupt their line of discourse through the insertion of apothegms, if not to clinch a point or strengthen an argument? Proverbs are presumed, by the speaker and usually by the public, to have persuasive power. The fact that they often are stated as simple observations merely increases their power of persuasion through the appearances of objectivity. They are quotable, of course, because they embody "wisdom," because they appeal to the self-interest of the audience. This provides a nonjudgmental definition of wisdom sayings as simply whatever someone feels important enough to quote, whatever the tradition presents as wise.

Since proverbs have a presumption of *authority,* we began Chapter 3 by noting that, especially when presented as simple assertions, they are powerful weapons in the wrong hands. No less than sages, scoundrels and fools also resort to proverbs in order to bolster an argument by appeal to consensus. The brief dialogues of thieves in the Anchos tale illustrate this point. In the first instance the thieves contrive their own "wisdom" saying to justify the killing; later, they sarcastically quote the words of the murdered sage, which becomes yet another pseudowisdom saying. In a similar way the prophet Ezekiel is sarcastically referred to as a "maker of proverbs" (*memashel meshalim,* Ezek 21:5).

3. Wisdom and Experience

The mysterious complexity of our life is not to be embraced by maxims.
                                        —George Eliot

Like the sages themselves, this study does not argue the substitution of logic for faith but rather the necessary support that faith derives (or should) from critical thinking. Wisdom's values are always regarded as of primary importance, but by insisting that they always be considered in relation to worldly values the sages dignified not only thinking but also the daily, existential context that such values clarify and that is their material support. In wisdom writing (Job, Kohelet), reflection upon human experience came center stage.

It should thus appear paradoxical that logical structures such as the quadripartite played an important role in the wisdom movement, since, as we noticed in the often playful elaboration of such structures, it becomes clear that the observations and even the recommendations of wisdom proverbs can be derived logically rather than from experience (with which they, I hope, correspond). Quadripartites constitute a class of proverbial expressions in which the primary motive seems to be neither aesthetic nor even valuational but experimental, as if the wisdom of experience could be explored, perhaps even generated, from the systematic exploration of all the virtualities of a given structure. It is thus necessary to qualify Cervantes's suggestion that proverbs are "short sentences drawn from long experience." Rather, at least in one important sense they are drawn from wisdom's own structures. In such experiments, where the goal is to discover as well as to teach, the contribution of the author seems to lie especially in the skillful use and elaboration upon a comprehensive formula, and such conventional frames are to be considered, in Abraham's (1983, 20) felicitous phrase, as "meaning-producing" structures. These are figures of thought rather than of speech, less literary structures than logical ones, less forms of expression than ways of thinking. And while in such experiments experience had indeed to be fitted to the requirements of logical patterns, it appears that experience emerges all the richer, at least in those cases where the patterns are all-inclusive and, indeed, generative of new insights and interpretations.

I would like to offer two further observations on the complex issue of wisdom's relation to experience, the first on the popular view that wisdom "encapsulates" experience. From the above one might rather conclude that wisdom evaluates experience and the *methods* of encapsulating it. Wisdom is thus analytic as opposed to simply assertive; it makes the crucial step beyond simple preference (the mere assertion of value) to its contextualization, and, further, it does not impose a particular context but rather the more general necessity of contextualization. Such a function is embryonically evident even at the structural level: the binary presentation of valuational topics is not only a stylistic event but also implies the view that value is best considered in relation to context (the context of other values) and, conversely, that contexts must always be discussed and evaluated. It thus represents a need to go beyond the naive habit of seeing things in isolation from either their value or the context of other values, as if, for example, haste is always wasteful or white always good or honesty always the best policy. For each of these, the sages retort that it all depends on its relation. The wisdom tradition has produced no finer statement of this *critical* relativism than Santob de Carrión's: "I can neither praise nor denounce a thing entirely, call it only beautiful or ugly. According to the circumstance and the nature of a thing, fast can be called slow and heads can be called tails" (Santob, lines 309–16).

My second observation concerns the relation between "proverb" and "saying" with which we began. Despite my wish to distinguish the terms, it must be stated that both function similarly with regards to experience. By this I mean that in interpretation and practical use both rely essentially on comparison, on analogy between the saying and a particular experiential situation that the saying seeks to clarify. This point may be missed because of differing modes of expression. On the one hand, for example, many proverbs occur as metaphors, what may be called a first level of analogy, with the result that the correct perception of the underlying general principle is often taken as the necessary and sufficient interpretation of the proverb. On the other hand, however, in teaching-sayings such as maxims the concrete or metaphorical stage is typically bypassed in favor of the general statement, thus eliminating the first level of analogy and placing the reflection at an abstract level. In both cases, however, behind each literal proposition there is a *sens connoté* (Crépeau 1975) to which it refers and that is its argument. In the Anchos tale the *sens littéral* is that "the birds are in heaven," but this only points (according to one reading) to the more general situation that "God is in heaven." Thus, the proverb "there is no smoke without fire" is translated as the general rule[17] that "all rumors have a basis in reality," which is then applied to a concrete, experiential situation. There is thus an analogy between two situations, as there always is in proverbs, but mediated by a general rule. This suggests that the main difference between proverbs and wisdom sayings (other than forms of expression, since the proverb is often metaphoric and, as previously noted, sententious) is that the former adds a further analogical step. Once the relation between the proverb and the general rule has been

---

17. Jason (1971, 621) calls this message-bearing aspect of proverbs their "idea": "the idea mediates between the multitude of particular contexts in social life and their poetic symbolization in the proverb. The metaphor in itself belongs already wholly to the realm of verbal art. In itself it has no relation to social reality. The idea relates the metaphor to social reality when the proverb is interpreted, i.e., applied to a particular social context."

perceived, however, then proverbs and wisdom sayings function in the same way, by both suggesting a further analogy with a situation, or, rather, by requiring the application of a general rule to a particular situation. Despite its often extreme conciseness, the proverb is an open form in that it constitutes a likeness with a situation external to itself; it requires comparison or particular application for its completion. This is why, in my view, it is best characterized by its biblical designation, *mashal* or comparison, since it implies by its very nature an analogy with an external situation.[18] Thus, quadripartite structures and their sayings always refer to experience; either directly or by implication, they require solution through interpretation or what Rad calls analogy with concrete situations.[19]

George Eliot may indeed be right in refusing to reduce our life's mystery to the rigid form of maxims, but this should not impede our awareness of the genre's great flexibility. For instance, we have often noticed the crucial role of oppositions in the creation of wisdom sayings, the virtual necessity of noticing "not X" as well as "X." However, one would prefer a more subtly graded perception of life's possibilities, perhaps by describing *positions* rather than simple *oppositions*. In charity, for example, between the topic "giving" and its opposite "not giving" real-life situations present many options: a stingy giving that is virtually a not-giving, an excessive generosity that actually destroys the capabilities of the giver, a giving of an acceptable sum but with an air of condescension, etc. Texts such as Abot 5:10 ("gives and takes") cannot consider such possibilities, and maxims with a different range or focus would be necessary. Here the concern is the assessment of attitudes or character types: "He that says, 'What is mine is yours and what is yours is your own'—he is *a saintly man;* and he that says, 'What is yours is mine, and what is mine is my own'—he is *a wicked man.*" However, it does not matter whether such pure types exist in nature, since they are ideal projections and goals of behavior, and the notation of *opposite* categories such as "give and not give" is simply an inclusive technique, a conceptual merism, one that implies all the intervening combinations or gradations, thus infinitely receptive to them all. Thus, to speak closer to real life, Maimonides advises one to consider himself or herself as neither wholly righteous nor completely wicked.

We may reflect further on this important point by reviewing the distinction between oppositions and contradictories. Take, for example, the notion

18. One must be cautious here, however, since in exegesis the term *mashal* is usually applied to literary form rather than to the use of such comparisons in their relation to experience.

19. On analogy, see G. von Rad (1972, 115–24); also Seitel (1969) and the excellent structural discussion in Grzybek (1987, 57–59).

of *profane,* which can be defined by its opposite: whatever is not holy. But "holy" cannot be defined by its simple opposite: what is not profane. For although what is not holy is profane, what is not profane is not necessarily and ipso facto and totally holy. Thus, from a holiness perspective "profane" is a contradictory, whereas from a profane perspective holy is an opposition (= not profane). Jean Baudrillard's distinction between an opposition and a disorder (= contradictory) will bring this into sharper focus: "Manicheism is the insurmountable antagonism between two powers; morality is only the opposition between two values. Thus, in the order of values there is always a possible reconciliation, whereas the disorder that reigns between the powers is uncompromising."[20] In terms of our own texts, this means that whereas righteous and wicked people occupy two irreconcilable orders, the behavioral values that allow them to participate in these orders are only oppositions; that is to say, they occupy different positions on the same continuum, so that increase in one (e.g., charity) also implies diminution of its opposite (stinginess). It is precisely the comparison of these values that allows the sages to make moral evaluations.

4. Wisdom and Happiness, At Least in the Long Run

Despite the prediction implied in wisdom proverbs, the world of the sages is projected not as one of necessity but of probability, and this impression is reinforced by the mode of observation, of stating what is *usually the case.* For example, just as wealth is more likely to be gained from diligent work than from laziness, moral habits also have their predictable results: "Poverty and shame are upon one who refuses discipline, but one who accepts reproof will be honored" (Prov 13:18). Note the limitation, however: He is honored but not necessarily made wealthy thereby. No text better clarifies the distinction between worldly and moral goods, between what we have termed **w**-values and **W**-values: the first result from work, the second from moral work. Good conduct does not necessarily lead to prosperity:

20. "Le manichéisme est l'antagonisme indépassable de deux puissances. La morale n'est que l'opposition de deux valeurs. Dans l'ordre des valeurs il y a toujours une réconciliation possible. Le désordre des puissances est irréconciliable" (Baudrillard 1987, 185). Analogously, for the Stoics there are two opposites to the sage: the student or philosopher and the nonsage. The first is partially a sage and thus only "not a sage," whereas the second is a contradictory.

Better a little with fear of the Lord than great treasure and turmoil with it. (Prov 15:16)

Better is a poor man who walks in his integrity than one who is perverse in speech and feels secure. (Prov 19:1)

Better a little with righteousness than great income without justice. (Prov 16:8)

One would like to agree with Bryce (1972b, 344) that such texts represent a violation of the traditional eudaemonistic interpretation of Proverbs. But the opposite may be the case: they may support such a view in their paradoxical observation that even a poor man, when he is morally superior, is better off than a wealthy one, at least in the long run. What is clear is that such texts, by remaining vague as to the ways in which morality is better, leave open such a possibility.

Another example of "observed" truth will allow us further to clarify the boundaries between observation of experience and didacticism:

Aujourd'hui en fleurs, demain en pleurs.
Today in flowers, tomorrow in tears.

One must resist the passive reading of such texts, for if this is viewed merely as a dejected observation on the passing of all things, then no wisdom teaching is perceived. However, even Ronsard in his most epicurean mood of "Mignonne, allons voir si la rose" used such an observation didactically, as a basis for argument:

(a) pleasure soon passes and
(b) is followed by permanent pain; therefore,
(c) apply this general principle to your present experience: "Since things are thus, *therefore* enjoy life while ye may."

Wisdom would follow the same tactic, except that it would perceive a further link of causality, this time between the two topics:

(a) pleasure in the present
(b) *causes* pain in the future; therefore . . .

Now the natural succession from pleasure to pain is read causally and the burden is shifted from a "ways of the world" perspective to a wisdom one:

your pleasure today will *cause* unhappiness tomorrow. The conclusion would be the reverse of Ronsard's, according to the principle that "Those who sow in tears reap with shouts of joy" (Ps 126:5), or, stated in terms of better-than: Tears today (since they will lead to joy tomorrow) are better than joy today (since it will lead to tears tomorrow, cf. Koh 7:1–8):

1. joy tomorrow (always) $(++)$
2. tears today (only) $(-+)$
3. joy today (only) $(+-)$
4. tears tomorrow (always) $(--)$

This paradigm allows us to describe a wisdom paradigm for causality: just as 3 leads to 4, 2 also leads to 1. In other words, causality functions between the first pair of propositions and between the second pair; but it never is operative between the two pairs. There is thus a barrier between the first pair of propositions and the second, and this barrier is insurmountable to causality. Thus, within the two groups causality functions in ascending order in the first group and in descending order in the second group.

More generally speaking and according to this view:

1. good conduct leads to good results
2. bad conduct leads to bad results

The problem arises, as we all know, when the good suffer and the wicked prosper (see Koh 8:14), when

3. good conduct leads to bad results!!
4. bad conduct leads to good results!!

Whereas the first two propositions express the Wisdom perspective, the second two articulate the "ways of the world," both the way things often happen and the judgments or evaluations of things that typically follow.

To give but one further example of this pervasive approach: "The name of the wicked will rot" (Prov 10:7b). The future tense of this saying is crucial to its wisdom meaning, its reference to what will be "in the long run"; in this respect the goals of the sages coincide with those of the prophets of Israel. By contrast, the conclusions of daily experience would be stated in the suppressed second part of the structure, namely, that the wicked may now triumph and the just are forgotten.

Thus it is that, despite its interest in adaptation to concrete living, wisdom's most common tactic is one of paradoxical opposition to the "ways of the world"[21] (but not to experience!), which are problematic to sages not only because of the mechanical indifference of the physical world but also and especially because of the unthinking acceptance of such a state of affairs as "true." Human judgment or "opinion" is seen to be at fault in its incorrect assessment of the workings of "the world" (Perry 1987b, 75), or in the confusion between facts and truths.[22] Thus, the observational mode of such a text as Kohelet has to be qualified, in the face of evidence to the contrary, by a faith that "in the long run" things will be (Koh 8:12) as the sage predicts.[23] This sense is conveyed by the simple future (as opposed to the present) tense, by the insistent focus on one's 'aḥarit or end (Prov 5:4, 11; 14:12; see Van Leeuwen 1990, 114) or that things happen in their (or God's, but not always our) time (Koh 3:11; Deut 11:14).

Wisdom thus establishes its ways according to rightness rather than consensus, by faith rather than observed cultural values. The possessors of this wisdom may be numerically more than one, but they are always a *minority* of many. The sages encountered many "facts of life," but these could have no standing until submitted to the scrutiny of Wisdom, until they were subjected to evaluation and the possibility of dissent. We have already noted how the quotation of a proverb entails a changing of the voice, a heightened tone, often an introductory formula such as "as the saying goes," or "as they say." One purpose of this break in the syntagmic line is to confer importance, to heighten the prestige and authority of the proverb. But in a wisdom context a no less important purpose is to register a disclaimer, a disagreement with another point of view, frequently unexpressed but always implied. This is in fact their chief interpersonal setting: Wisdom proverbs are always spoken as contradictions to another point of view.

21. I take the expression from Menachem ha-Meiri (on Prov 14:20–21).

22. Wisdom is thus resolutely opposed to current ethnocentric definitions of cultures (in the plural); that is to say, "styles de vie particuliers, non transmissibles, saisissibles sous forme de productions concrètes—techniques, moeurs, institutions, croyances—plutôt que de capacités virtuelles, et correspondant à des valeurs observables au lieu de vérités" (Lévi-Strauss 1983, 50; quoted in Finkielkraut 1987, 80). Such a distinction is valuable in understanding such texts as the creation narrative of Genesis, since its interest is not scientific fact (called "observable values" by Finkielkraut) but moral and spiritual truths.

23. One can, of course, view such statements as Koh 8:12–13 as mere pious glosses (Crenshaw 1987, 155), but it seems more accurate to view them as characteristic of the wisdom enterprise itself. More dissonant is Kohelet's criticism of the "long run" view in the previous verse: "It is because judgment is not quickly brought against evil that the hearts of human beings are full of wrongdoing" (Koh 8:11), an echo of Jonah's complaint that God is "slow to anger" (4:2).

Take, for example, any typical proverb of implication:

Jeunesse oiseuse, vieillesse disetteuse.

Easygoing youth, destitute old age.

Recall that the saying "Today in flowers, tomorrow in tears" may of course be taken as simply a jaded observation on the passing of all things. As a wisdom saying, however, such sayings are reminders to those who think and act as if good times are eternally guaranteed. Their proverb would be: "Easygoing youth, easygoing old age!"

Or take the following observation:

Dans un vieux pot on fait de la bonne soupe.

You can make good soup in an old pot.

However, this can also be read as a wisdom warning, a condemnation of the usual point of view, here a bias in favor of newness and the corresponding prejudice against things old as would be expressed in the hypothetical saying:

Dans un vieux pot on fait de la mauvaise soupe.

In an old pot you make bad soup.

And, by implication: "In a new pot you can make good soup."

No sequence better makes this point than the following:

A pauper is hated even by his neighbor, but a rich man has many friends.

He who despises his neighbor is a sinner, but happy is he who is kind to the poor. (Prov 14:20–21)

In order to make the wisdom argument perfectly clear, either the first verse should be put in quotes in order to stress that it is a different opinion, or the second verse should be preceded by a disclaimer such as "But I say." At any rate, the second takes strong objection to the normal ways of the world as expressed in the first verse, to the way people tend to regard the poor and rich.

5. Wisdom and God

Kohelet's balancing of plus and minus values in chap. 3 (see Chapter 3.2.a) is preceded by the pointed remark that "There is a time for each *ḥepets,* each desire," arguing that it is the time that confers value. That is to say, desires are not relational; when I desire to speak I do not also normally experience a desire to be silent. But it is the relational context, the possibility of its opposite, that gives the desire moral meaning. As Saussure argued, therefore, meaning is relational to its opposite. There is a second and more global sense of context/relation as well: the total context that encloses both terms. Thus, when Kohelet asserts (4:2) that "The dead is better than the living, but better than both...," this third term is, from the human point of view, an impossibility, a straining of logical limits, but it *is* to be included among God's possibilities of action.

From the contextualization and relativization of values, it does not follow that *all* is relative and that no absolute values exist. Quite the opposite, God as the ground of being allows the perspective of relativity (all is vanity *under* the sun perhaps, but *above* it?). Just as each day is not absolute in its independence but derives its limitation from the Sabbath, each finite thing is relative because it can be referred to God and *is not* God. God is thus, as it were, the guarantor of the relativity of things and values, and things can be dissolved or turned into their opposites.

The passage from observation to faith and from a purely natural to a more general perspective is in evidence even in such a passage as Sirach 38:24–39:11, which extends its sympathy even to the practical arts. The sages are judged to be superior, nevertheless, because "they understand the workings of this world." This is not intended to justify contemplative withdrawal, quite the contrary, for the sage is involved in the workings of government (38:33). But he also "reflects on the teachings of the Most High" (39:1). The attempt to clarify the relation between the sage and God, as well as between wisdom literature and revelation, seems to be the explanation of two apparently oppositional proverbs:

> *The fear of the Lord* is a fountain of life, that one may avoid the snares of death. (Prov 14:27)

> *The teaching of the wise* is a fountain of life, that one may avoid the snares of death. (Prov 13:14)

That is to say, both proverbs are true because the sage cultivates a consciousness that perceives both the relativity of the workings of this world and also their real value.

CONCLUSION

1. The Need to Interpret

In paremiology the rapprochement with folklore and its democratic ideals has led us astray.[1] Since wisdom is an intellectually aristocratic movement, it believes that whatever has currency among the folk is not for that very reason to be considered wise—indeed, may be cause for suspicion. The tradition insisted that sages are special people, that their actions and especially their speech actions are meaningful. This is the point of the Anchos story: not only the assertion of value, not even the categorization of mankind as located between wise and foolish (which has only propaganda value until a content is made clearer), nor even the analysis and comparison of values, as important as this is, but the *interpretation* of Anchos's "wise" behavior, which cannot even be perceived as wise until it is interpreted.

To state the matter from a different perspective, in folk

---

1. For example, Hasan-Rokem's continued insistence on an earlier definition, according to which a proverb is "a genre of folk literature . . . referring to collective experience" (Hasan-Rokem and Alexander 1988, 1). Similarly, Krikman (1985, 59) refers to the popular conception of the proverb as lying "just somewhere on the borderlands between language and folklore."

proverbs it is assumed that, being an induction from individual cases (see Jason in Fontaine 1982, 49), the original message is clear to everyone—it is "current" because it is understood. In wisdom as exemplified by the Anchos story, the original experience is unique and unclear, and the meaning can arise only through interpretation. It might even be said that a sage's word is one that sets out to provoke an interpretive response. I refer to this elsewhere as the "sharpness" of wisdom sayings, their need of interpretation and dialogue: "Iron sharpens iron, and one man sharpens another" (Prov 27:17). The purpose of the sharpening is not that the two blades may resemble one another but rather that the newly sharpened one may also be able to cut, to become what Barthes (1980, 31) called a sharp "knife of value."

2. Lowly Containers

By way of conclusion, let us review the structural method by offering several further applications. First, let us return to our initial metaphor of how containers can affect their contents. The avowed purpose of the following anecdote is to prove that words of wisdom can be preserved only in lowly vessels:

> ... the story of the daughter of a Roman emperor [Hadrian], who said to Rabbi Joshua ben Hananiah: "What brilliant wisdom in such an ugly vessel!" Whereupon he exclaimed: "Oh, you daughter of a man who puts wine in vessels of clay!" "Wherein should he put it?" she asked. "You nobles should put it in vessels of gold and silver!" Whereupon she went home and told her father, who ordered the wine to be put into vessels of gold and silver, and the wine became sour. They then went to Rabbi Joshua and asked him, "Why did you give her such advice?" "As she spoke to me, so I spoke to her," Rabbi Joshua replied. "But there are also handsome people that are learned!" they said. "If the same people were ugly, they would be still more learned," was Rabbi Joshua's answer. (BT Ta'anit 7a–b)

In this amusing example the less savory implications of structure have to be played out before proper adjustments or new understandings are produced.

At the first level, the daughter learns the limitations of the first bit of wisdom at her own expense. Here, her failure of insensitivity is doubled (rewarded?) by a failure of interpretation: she is unable to see the analogy between Rabbi Joshua's pedagogical (and vindictive?) advice and her own remark, for from Joshua's paradigm:

> lowly container > good wine

she should have learned:

> precious containers > bad (spoiled) wine

At this point, however, the narrator injects the outraged voice of experience, according to which one can indeed find:

> good wine + precious containers!

Of course, Rabbi Joshua might agree, but that is not the point, since such a reading weakly substitutes a simple juxtaposition of terms for the sage's insistence on causality; the point of his teaching is that it is only the lowly container that is appropriate to fine wine because anything more precious might alter the contents. His view is not verifiable—one cannot compare what is with what might have been—and the proof or confirmation by experience must be postponed to the future, to what will happen "in the long run."

Thus it is that lowly proverbs (and lowly sages!) come to preserve wisdom's precious liquid. But just as the container has shaped the contents, the clear liquid points beyond itself:

> [The Sages] bequeathed their pure wisdom in writing, *distilling it* without any bodily mixture . . .
>
> For this reason alone every sensible person wants to see the sages, but not through their bodily shape. (Santob, lines 1277–80, 1285–88)

But their bodily shape is words, and one needs to know how to see through words!

3. Spare the Words and Spoil the Child

I have proposed that wisdom is an art form in which art is nevertheless subservient to meaning or moral values—thus, more accurately, a thought form. I have further tried to suggest how these values can be accessed through attention to the deep structure of wisdom sayings as they are artfully rendered through the forms and words of proverbs. The next example shows both that wisdom is hardly a matter of mere words or even structures, and also that words are (virtually) the entire matter of wisdom: "He who spares the rod hates his son, but he who loves him is diligent to discipline him" (Prov 13:24 [RSV]). The part of the verse that is of usual interest is the first half, perhaps because of the well-known English poetical rendering: "Spare the rod and spoil the child." According to the usual reading, the verse seems to recommend corporal punishment. But those involved in parenting or education might legitimately ask for more precision: when is physical punishment recommended? Always? Twice a day? Every hour? Surely only when necessary, although the verse doesn't say so. Indeed, it seems to have a more systematic approach in mind: if you don't do this, then you are a child-hater.[2]

Our new habits of reading should be able to help at this point. First of all, one should want to know whether the only alternative to "hates his son" is "loves his son." Can there experientially or even logically be no intermediate stages between the two? Second, we seem to be dealing here with a case of what is fondly known as "antithetical parallelism," as exemplified by the neat opposition "hates his son" and "loves his son." But we have learned that such oppositions often occur in pairs, and our attention should now be on the lookout for the second pair of opposites. This is nearly impossible in the present case, not because they do not exist but because our usual translations have the support of the nearly sacred authority of the principle of "semantic parallelism," which in the present case enforces the synonymy of the two halves of the verse, and more particularly the italicized words: "He who *spares the rod* hates his son, but he who loves him is diligent to *discipline* him." In fact, however, although these expressions share the idea of correction, in this proverb they are opposites: the first refers to physical punishment as exemplified by the *shebet* or stick, and the

---

2. Exegetically, however, the only thing that might trouble such a reader is the question as to whether the statement is definitional or whether it simply gives an illustration. In other words, is sparing the rod merely an example of the kind of behavior that might lead one to say: "he hates his son"? Or is such behavior definitional: sparing the rod is what is really meant by "hating one's son"; it is that behavior that best defines this kind of person.

second refers to a different and milder form of correction, *musar,* verbal chastisement.[3]

We now begin to sense the parameters of the problem under discussion. With the help of our quadripartite structure we become aware of the four possible behaviors and the order of their recommendation:

1. give / verbal chastisement $(++)$ = love
2. give / physical chastisement $(+-)$ = not hate
3. withhold / verbal chastisement $(-+)$ = not love
4. withhold / physical chastisement $(--)$ = hate

The matter must be explored through the complex relation between the first and second halves of the verse. Exegetically, we are not allowed to view the second half as merely a restatement of the first or as a limp gloss. On the contrary, it "goes one better" by setting the entire problem in a larger framework. Notice that the first half is not rejected, for whoever adds the crucial second half allows that physical punishment may be necessary. Analogously, Mosaic legislation recognized the desperate case of the "rebellious son" (Deut 21:18–21), but the Rabbis were quick to state that even here the value was admonitory and that such a persecution in fact never took place (BT Sanhedrin 71a). The procedure was rather an object-lesson, something held up to children as an admonishment. Thus one can suggest that what is withheld is not only the actual punishment but "the rod," that is to say, the threat, since clearly rods can be used to threaten as well as to hit, and the latter, the striking of one's own child, may in fact have been inconceivable to parents. The reading of the worst case would thus be: he who fails even to threaten physical punishment . . .

Working up the ladder from worst to best, we next come to the lack of love as exemplified by withholding *verbal* correction. Recall David's failures regarding his son Adonijah: "His father had never at any time scolded him by asking: 'Why have you done thus and so?'" (1 Kgs 1:6). The next stage up would be to apply the *warning* or threat of physical punishment that is withheld in the worst stage or stage four.

What then is ideal behavior with regard to one's child? Not only diligence, as specified by the RSV text, but also the crucial detail rendered in the NJV version: "He who loves him disciplines him *early.*" Education, if it is to be gentle and avoid the radical threat of physical punishment, must begin early

3. In late Hebrew *musar* refers only to verbal correction, but already in Scripture this meaning is prominent: they are reproofs (Prov 6:23) that are heard (Prov 1:8; 8:33; 19:27; Deut 4:36; Job 4:3–4).

in life, and the mere possibility of more cruel intervention later is already a sign of parental neglect.

I pause a bit on this verse because an overemphasis on its exemplary technical or aesthetic qualities can be misleading. I refer to Robert Alter's otherwise excellent focus (1985, 167) on wisdom as a language craft, to the extent that in his view it is an attention to the *form* of this verse that leads us "to see what it means in moral consequences truly to love or hate one's son." I suggest, however, that it is also necessary, morally speaking, to focus on wisdom as a thought craft and to ask why this verse is so compelling not only poetically but intellectually and morally. This involves especially the search for and perception of crucial semantic oppositions.

Let me summarize by asking why these exegetical and structural gymnastics are necessary. In what way can they possibly affect my behavior? Pedagogically and morally speaking, what is to be gained from another interpretation of what everyone seems to know, or that popular wisdom would have us believe: that it is sometimes necessary to use physical punishment?[4] A great deal. First of all, I wonder how many irate parents have received moral support and encouragement for child abuse from such an abusive reading, from the facile implication that if I don't punish my child then I don't love him or her? Here the verse comes to teach essential wisdom values. First it encourages us to reflect that "not hating" is not necessarily "loving," that there are other alternatives, and that physical punishment is therefore *not* the highest form of love, perhaps not even loving at all. It also teaches that the usual rendering of the Hebrew text is ill-conceived, and that a more accurate rendering would be: "Spare the *words* and spoil the child." The sages used artful contrivance not as an end in itself but as means to more effective moral teaching and thinking and acting, and it matters greatly if we pause in delight over the exquisite ballet of words and go on beating our children or, worse, use those very artfully crafted words as leave to do so. After all, the sages argued that "death and life are in the power of the tongue" (Prov 18:21), and this is more serious still than a "neat little choreography" (Alter 1985, 167) of words.

---

4. Twain's aunt Polly tries to justify herself in this way: "Spare the rod and spile the child, as the Good Book says." But then she speaks from her own heart's wisdom: "I ain't got the heart to lash him somehow ..., and every time I hit him my old heart most breaks" (Twain, 1982, 10).

APPENDIX: ABOT 5:10–15[1]

In citing historical examples of full quadripartite structures above, I desisted from quoting the entire string of such sayings in Mishnah Abot 5:10–15, and I complete the series here for the sake of reference. To my knowledge, this text represents the most thoroughgoing usage of quadripartite sayings in all of literature and is thus the clearest possible instance of experimental play with the logical possibilities of deep structure. Further, their arrangement in a typical "string" is a benefit to analysis as well as to memorization. One should especially note that each example of the string occurs in a completely elaborated-upon structure, whereas in typical cases studied above the quadripartite was implicit and had to be generated.

> There are four types of character: easy to provoke and easy to appease—his loss is canceled by his gain; hard to provoke and hard to appease—his gain is canceled by his loss; hard to provoke and easy to appease—he is a saintly man; easy to provoke and hard to appease—he is a wicked man. (Abot 5:11)

This Mishnah has the same structure as the previous one: $(-+/+-/++/--)$. Again, the $(-+)$ proposition is "better than" the $(+-)$ one, meaning that that culture places a higher value on softness than hardness in such matters. Although, mathematically speaking, $(-+)$ and $(+-)$ should both equal zero, the language of this Mishnah is precious in its confirmation of the stronger value of the second member, so that $(-+)$ indicates a somewhat positive character in that the negative is canceled by a gain.

---

1. For Abot 5:10 see Chapter 1.1.

> There are four types of disciple: swift to learn and swift to forget —
> his gain is canceled by his loss; slow to learn and slow to forget — his
> loss is canceled by his gain; swift to learn and slow to forget — this is
> a happy lot; slow to learn and swift to forget — this is an evil lot. (Abot
> 5:12)

This text varies the first two members: $(+-/-+)$, thereby retaining the
chiasmus of the first pair; the second pair remains the same: $(++/--)$. In
terms of the typologies being proposed in these texts, this Mishnah, along
with 5:15, is peculiar in that the moral categories depend neither on attitudes
(e.g., "easy to appease") nor on identifiable actions such as "saying and
giving" but rather on what seems to be inherited abilities, a point that
Bertinoro raises in his commentary on the Mishnah (first published in Venice,
1548–49): "*This is an evil lot:* It would not have been appropriate for the
Mishnah here to speak of 'righteous' or 'wicked,' since this matter does not
depend upon man's free choice but rather on a deficiency that was his from
his creation." Alternatively, the Mishnah may wish to address precisely this
point and to assert that these qualities do, to a certain degree, depend on
human effort.

> There are four types of almsgivers: he that is minded to give but not
> that others should give — he is stingy with what belongs to others; he
> that is minded that others should give but not that he should give — he
> is stingy with what belongs to himself; he that is minded to give and
> also that others should give — he is a saintly man; he that is minded not
> to give and that others should not give — he is a wicked man. (Abot
> 5:13)

This text has the same structure as the preceding, with the slight variant in
the statement of proposition 2, upsetting the chiasmus. Thus proposition 1
states $(+-)$ and proposition 2 states $(+-)$. This is rather atypical of such
structures in that it renders inconclusive the assertion of "better than," and
one cannot discern whether 1 is preferable to 2 or not. This would seem to
suggest that, in the eyes of the author of this Mishnah, stinginess is a negative
quality in equal degree as applied to another or to one's self, it being
impossible to assert the superiority of another self over one's own self, as one
might expect from some "wisdom" sets of values.[2]

2. This is consistent with Rabbi Judah the Prince's principle that both selves must always be
considered, one's own and that of one's neighbor (see Chapter 3, n. 25).

> There are four types among them that frequent the House of Study: he that goes and does not practice—he has the reward of his going; he that practices but does not go—he has the reward of his practicing; he that goes and practices—he is a saintly man; he that neither goes nor practices—he is a wicked man. (Abot 5:14)

This text has the same structure as the preceding. In these two texts the $(+ -/ + -)$ structure of what would normally be the better-than components suggests that there is really no preference of one over the other and the better-than does not apply in these cases. Indeed, in such matters as giving charity it is important both to give and to wish others to give, just as in fulfilling the commandments one can find texts to justify the priority of both learning and deeds, leading to the conclusion that both are necessary and interdependent. It is of interest that in the latter text as opposed to the preceding one, the valuation of the intermediate positions is positive in that both mention only the (partial) reward, perhaps as encouragement for each good thing. However, the order of the first two statements mirrors the order of topics, and both may carry a suggestion of preference, namely that one must "go" in order to "practice"; from this one might be led to conclude that although the person described in proposition 1 may be on a lesser level in that he only learns and does not practice, in the long run he may come to practice and thus end up ahead of proposition 2, who practices now but may soon forget to do so through lack of learning.

> There are four types among them that sit in the presence of the Sages: the sponge, the funnel, the strainer, and the sifter. "The sponge"—which soaks up everything; "the funnel"—which takes in at this end and lets out at the other end; "the strainer"—which lets out the wine and collects the lees; "the sifter"—which extracts the coarsely ground flour and collects the fine flour. (Abot 5:15)

This may be restated as follows:

1.	he retains good and bad	$(+ -)$
2.	he forgets both good and bad	$(- +)$
3.	he forgets the good and retains the bad	$(- -)$
4.	he retains the good and forgets the bad	$(+ +)$

In this final text the commentary, which evaluates the four propositions, is not only included, as in the previous cases, but actually precedes the descriptive portion. According to our previous analyses, this text proposes that $(-+)$ is "better than" $(+-)$, suggesting that retaining the bad is so serious that it is better to forget it even if this means also forgetting the good. One must constantly bear in mind, however, that in conjunctive structures (the terms are joined by "and"), as opposed to possessive ones, the predicate or second term of each proposition is more an equal than a determinant member, with the result that the better-than statements do not necessarily have the $(-+)$ and $(+-)$ sequence. Even here, however, this sequence is the usual case since, as stated above, in our languages the predicate usually occupies the second position.

As to the sequence of propositions in this quadripartite string, in all except the final example the concluding members 3 and 4 take the form $(++/--)$. This is in keeping with the spirit of better-than teachings, which offer the positive before the negative and like to conclude with the "worse." The inversion of 3 and 4 in the last text seems to reflect an axiomatic refusal in Jewish teaching to end a series on a sour note. This abrupt structural inversion thus signals the end of the series.[3]

---

3. This is also the case in Koh 3:8; see Chapter 3.2(a).

SIGLA AND TECHNICAL TERMS

These "definitions" are really descriptions, not written in the heavens but rather induced from historical examples of the quadripartite, thus empirical rather than either systematic or dogmatic or even theoretical. Moreover, their value is mainly heuristic, intending not to assert universal applicability but rather to test usefulness and possible range of application. Unless I am mistaken, such an approach characterizes even such entrenched Greimasians as Daniel Patte, in his call both to multiply heuristic methods and to renounce our desire for methodology for its own sake. At any rate, these descriptions are presented both as reference and as an introduction to the analytical vocabulary of the above study.

+   Designates a topic as having positive value according to the text in which it occurs and the culture or point of view to which it refers. Broadly, "+" values are "good" and praiseworthy and desirable.

−   Designates a topic as having negative value according to the text in which it occurs and the culture or point of view to which it refers. Broadly, "−" values are "bad" and disparaged and undesirable.

Binary (see also **Proposition**)   Having *two* terms or topics. In this study Binary refers mainly to Propositions.

Commentary   The moral evaluation or interpretation of a proposition, usually by seeking to identify the situation described in the proverb or saying. The commentary may become incorporated into the saying, as in Abot 5:10–15, or it may be explicitly appended, or it may be simply expected in the act of interpretation.

Contextualization   In my model of quadripartite structure, this refers to the binary structure of propositions; that is, the habit of viewing a single topic within the *context* of another topic, typically a **W**-value within the context of a **w**-value, or vice versa. In this book the term does *not* refer to the context of performance, that is, the social setting or background within which a proverb originates or is performed. Nor does it refer to the broader literary context that integrates or at least contains individual sayings, such as anthologies or collections.

In the Long Run   This is a common justification for **Wisdom** values, promising that, often as against the current lowly status of the Wise as perceived in daily experience, benefit or happiness or some other positive result will accrue. Thus, one can be advised to "cast your bread upon the waters, *since* in the long run you will recover it" (Koh 11:1; RSV: "for you will find it after many days").

Logical Connectives   A word or words that specify a logical relationship between the (two) topics of a proposition; the particular logical relationship according to which two topics are juxtaposed and related (see **Semantic Relatedness**). Four are discussed here: causation or "Act/Consequence Relationship," equivalence (identificational/contrastive), conjunction ("and"), possession ("of").

Opposition/Opposite   As used here, this term is applied to valuational topics rather than to propositions. It indicates the negation of a valuational topic. For example, the valuational topic "taking" has "not taking" as its opposite; conversely, the opposite of "not taking" is "taking." Moreover, the opposite of "good" is "not good," although, in the generation of oppositions, the contradictory "bad" can often be considered its equivalent. Note carefully that, whereas individual valuational topics do not distinguish "not good" and "bad" (both being negative), such a distinction is operative between or among propositions, thus allowing more finely nuanced comparisons.

Popular   The term is used here not in a sociological sense but rather to indicate a function, that of simple assertion of values as opposed to their analysis. When a proverb of simple preference (q.v.) is used to contradict another, however, then the second assertion may already be viewed as exercising a critical function.

Proposition (see also **Binary**)   A statement of value consisting of the juxtaposition of two terms or topics logically related (joined by a logical connective). Note that propositions need not state actual proverbs as they are performed. For example, Saint Paul's "it is better to marry than to burn" implies *two* propositions: (a) it is better to marry and not burn, than (b) not to marry and burn.

Proverb   A primary structure of valuation.

(Proverb of) Simple Preference   The assertion that one value (whether

W or **w**) is "better than" its negation or its opposite. Note carefully that typical better-than sayings or proverbs are constructed from proverbs of simple preference but are *not* of that category. For example, "it is better to be poor than wicked" assumes the following:

1. rich is better than poor
2. righteous is better than wicked.

The contextualization of one by the other, however, is not at all simple preference but rather what we have called a wisdom saying or proverb. See also **Popular**.

Quadripartite   Having *four* parts. This refers to the historical occurrence of structures (sayings) having four propositions. It also proposes that sayings and proverbs not explicitly composed of four propositions can be fruitfully studied by reference to such a structure, which can be reconstructed from the givens of the saying.

Saying   This term is not used with any rigor here. Its main use is to indicate a statement less succinct than a proverb or aphorism. Thus, a full quadripartite is a saying but not a proverb.

Semantic Relatedness   This describes the appropriate degree of meaningful relation between the two topics (or their opposites) of a proposition or saying, typically the **W** and the **w** values. For example, two topics may be complementary, as "it is better to *give* than to *receive*." Or they may be potentially contradictory, as when things "appear good and are bad."

Simple Preference   See (**Proverb of**) **Simple Preference.**

Topic (see **Valuational Topic**)   The terms of a saying or proverb, what it is about, the values it asserts. I proceed on the assumption that all topics are valuational.

Valuational Topic (see also **Topic**)   The valuation (assertion of a value) and/or evaluation of a topic is usually expressed in "+" and/or "−" values.

W   This designates a major **W**isdom value (e.g., righteousness, life, wisdom, peace), hence one having absolute worth (albeit typically contextualized).

w   This designates a **w**orldly value (according to the "ways of the world"), hence a value that is never absolute but varies according to context and situation (e.g., wealth, health, power, good manners).

Ways of the world   See **w**.

Wisdom Saying   A primary (i.e., binary) structure of valuation (or asserting value) and evaluation (the use to which that saying can be put to compare values and establish their relative priority). Its binary composition typically contextualizes a **W** value with a **w** value.

SELECTED BIBLIOGRAPHY

Abrahams, Roger D.
  1968 "Introductory Remarks to a Rhetorical Theory of Folklore." *Journal of American Folklore* 81:143–58.
  1972 "Proverbs and Proverbial Expressions." In *Folklore and Folklife: An Introduction.* Edited by Richard M. Dorson. Chicago: University of Chicago Press, 117–43.
  1983 "Open and Closed Forms in Moral Tales." In *Studies in Aggadah and Jewish Folklore.* Edited by I. Ben-Ami and Joseph Dan. Jerusalem: Magnes, 19–33.
Alter, Robert
  1985 *The Art of Biblical Poetry.* New York: Basic Books.
Amalfi, Gaetano
  1896 "Die Kraniche des Ibykus in der Sage." *Zeitschrift des Vereins für Volkskunde* 6:115–29.
Andriantsilaniarivo, E.
  1982 "Hain-teny." In *Cahiers Jean Paulhan 2.* Paris: Gallimard, 274–85.
Babylonian Talmud
  1935–48 Edited by I. Epstein. London: Soncino.
Barley, Nigel
  1972 "A Structural Approach to the Proverb and Maxim." *Proverbium* 20:737–50.
Barthes, Roland
  1970 *S/Z.* Paris: Seuil.
  1972 *Le Degré zéro de l'écriture.* Paris: Seuil.
  1980 *Roland Barthes par Roland Barthes.* Paris: Seuil.
Battesti, Jean
  1974 "Proverbes et aphorismes dans le *Conde Lucanor* de Don Juan de Manuel." In *Hommage à André Joucla-Ruau.* Département d'études hispaniques. Aix-en-Provence: Université de Provence, 1–61.
Baudrillard, Jean
  1987 *Cool Memories.* Paris: Galilée.
Beaujot, Jean-Pierre
  1984 "Le Travail de la définition dans quelques maximes de La Rochefoucauld." In *Les Formes brèves de la prose et le discours discontinu (XVIe–XVIIe siècles).* Edited by Jean Lafond. Paris: Vrin, 95–100.
Berlin, Adele
  1985 *The Dynamics of Biblical Parallelism.* Bloomington: Indiana University Press.
Bocados de oro
  1879 In *Mittheilungen aus dem Escurial.* Edited by Hermann Knust. Tübingen: Literarischer Verein.

1958 Abu-l-Wafaʾ Al-Mubassir Ibn Fatik, *Mujtar al Hikam.* Edited by ʾA. Badawiy. Madrid: Publicaciones del Instituto Egipcio de Estudios Islámicos.

1971 *Romanistische Versuche und Vorarbeiten,* no. 37. Edited by M. Crombach. Bonn: Romanische Seminar der Universität Bonn.

Bolte, Johannes, and Georg Polivka
1963 *Ammerkungen zu den Kinder- und Hausmärchen der Brüder Grimm.* 5 vols. Hildesheim: Ohlms. (Originally published Leipzig, 1913–32)

Bryce, G. E.
1972a "Another Wisdom 'Book' in Proverbs." *Journal of Biblical Literature* 91:145–57.
1972b " 'Better'-Proverbs: An Historical and Structural Study." In *Book of Seminar Papers,* no. 2. Edited by L. C. McGaughy. Missoula, Mont.: Society of Biblical Literature, 343–54.

Calila y Dimna
1984 Edited by J. M. Cacho Blecua and María Jesús Lacarra. Madrid: Castalia.

Camp, Claudia V.
1985 *Wisdom and the Feminine in the Book of Proverbs.* Sheffield: *JSOT* Press.

Castigos y documentos para bien vivir
1952 Edited by Agapito Rey. Indiana University Humanities Series, no. 24. Bloomington: Indiana University Press.

La Celestina
1969 Edited by Dorothy S. Severin. Madrid: Alianza.

Cram, D.
1983 "The Linguistic Status of the Proverb." *Cahiers de Lexicologie* 43:53–71.

Crenshaw, James L.
1976 (editor) *Studies in Ancient Israelite Wisdom.* New York: Ktav.
1981 *Old Testament Wisdom.* Atlanta, Ga.: John Knox.
1987 *Ecclesiastes: A Commentary.* The Old Testament Library. Philadelphia: Westminster.

Crépeau, Pierre
1975 "La Définition du proverbe." *Fabula* 16:285–304.

Devoto, Daniel
1972 *Introducción al estudio de Don Juan Manuel y en particular de "El Conde de Lucanor."* Madrid: Castalia.

Dundes, Alan
1981 "On the Structure of the Proverb." In Mieder and Dundes 1981:43–64. (Originally published in *Proverbium* 25 [1975]:961–73)

Ethics of the Fathers. *See* Pirkei Abot.

Faur, José
1986 *Golden Doves with Silver Dots.* Bloomington: Indiana University Press.

Finkielkraut, Alain
1987 *La Défaite de la pensée.* Paris: Gallimard.

Flores de filosofía
1878 In *Dos obras didácticas y dos leyendas.* Edited by H. Knust. Madrid: Sociedad de Bibliófilos, 17:1–83.

Fontaine, Carole R.
1982 *Traditional Sayings in the Old Testament.* Sheffield: Almond.

Fox, Michael V.
1989 *Qohelet and His Contradictions.* Sheffield: Almond.

Gammie, John G., and Leo G. Perdue (editors)
1990 *The Sage in Israel and the Ancient Near East.* Winona Lake, Ind.: Eisenbrauns.

Gaster, Moses
  1934 *Ma 'aseh Book (Book of Jewish Tales and Legends)* Vol. 1 of 2 vols. Philadelphia: Jewish Publication Society.
Genette, Gérard
  1966 *Figures I.* Paris: Seuil.
Golopentia-Eretescu, Sanda
  1965 "La Structure linguistique des proverbes équationnels." *Cahiers de linguistique théorique et appliquée* 2:63–69.
  1972 "What Is Right Is Right." *Semiotica* 5:118–61.
Gordis, Robert
  1968 *Koheleth—The Man and His World: A Study of Ecclesiastes.* New York: Schocken.
Greimas, Algirdas Julien
  1970 *Du Sens.* Paris: Seuil.
  1987 *On Meaning.* Translated by Paul J. Perron and Frank H. Collins. Minneapolis: University of Minnesota Press. Foreword by Fredric Jameson.
Grésillon, Almuth, and Dominique Maingueneau
  1989 "Polyphonie, proverbe et détournement." *Langages* 73:112–25.
Grzybek, Peter
  1987 "Foundations of Semiotic Proverb Study." *Proverbium* 4:39–85.
Hasan-Rokem, Galit
  1974 "Riddle and Proverb. The Relationship Exemplified by an Aramaic Proverb." *Proverbium* 24:192–204.
  1983 "The Proverb as a Key to Plot Complexity" (in Hebrew). In *Studies in Aggadah and Jewish Folklore.* Edited by Issachar Ben-Ami and Joseph Dan. Jerusalem: Magnes, 367–97.
Hasan-Rokem, Galit, and Tamar Alexander
  1988 "Games of Identity in Proverb Usage: Proverbs of a Sephardic-Jewish Woman." *Proverbium* 5:1–14.
Havelock, Eric A.
  1963 *Preface to Plato.* Cambridge: Harvard University Press.
Hildebrandt, Ted
  1988 "Proverbial Pairs: Compositional Units in Proverbs 10–29." *Journal of Biblical Literature* 107:207–24.
Hoglund, Kenneth G.
  1987 "The Fool and the Wise in Dialogue." In *The Listening Heart: Essays in Wisdom and the Psalms in Honor of Roland E. Murphy.* Edited by Kenneth G. Hoglund, Elizabeth F. Huwiler, Jonathan T. Gass, and Roger W. Lee. *JSOT* Supplement Series, no. 58. Sheffield: Sheffield Academic Press, 161–80.
Honein Ibn Isaac
  1896a *Musrei ha-Filosofim.* Edited by A. Loewenthal. Translated by Yehuda Al-Harisi. Berlin: Kauffmann.
  1896b *Sinnsprüche der philosophen* (German translation of the *Musrei ha-Filosofim*). Translated by A. Loewenthal. Berlin: Calvary.
Ibn Gabirol, Solomon
  1925 *Choice of Pearls.* Translated by A. Cohen. New York: Block.
Jacobs, Louis
  1978 "The Relationship Between Religion and Ethics in Jewish Thought." In *Contemporary Jewish Ethics.* Edited by Menachem Mark Kellner. New York: Sanhedrin, 41–57. Reprinted from *Religion and Morality.* Edited by Gene Outka and John P. Reeder. Doubleday, 1973: 157–72.

Jameson, Fredric
1972 *The Prison-House of Language.* Princeton: Princeton University Press.
Japhet, Sara
1985 *The Commentary of R. Samuel Ben Meir Rashbam on Qoheleth.* Jerusalem: Magnes.
Jason, Heda
1971 "Proverbs in Society: The Problem of Meaning and Function." *Proverbium*
17:617–23.
Jobling, David
1986a *The Sense of Biblica Narrative I.* Sheffield: *JSOT* Supplement Series, no. 7.
1986b *The Sense of Biblica Narrative II.* Sheffield: *JSOT* Supplement Series, no. 39.
Jolles, André
1958 *Einfache Formen.* Darmstadt: Niemeyer.
Juan Manuel
1979 *El conde Lucanor.* Edited by José Manuel Blecua. Madrid: Castalia.
1983 *El conde Lucanor.* In *Obras completas.* Edited by José Manuel Blecua. 2 vols.
Madrid: Gredos, 1982, 1983; 2:19–491.
Keil, Yehudah (editor)
1983 The Book of Proverbs (in Hebrew). Jerusalem: Mossad Harav Kook.
Kirshenblatt-Gimblet, Barbara
1981 "Towards a Theory of Proverb Meaning." In Mieder and Dundes 1981:111–21.
(Originally published in *Proverbium* 22 [1973]:821–27)
Knust, Hermann
1878 (editor) *Dos obras didácticas y dos leyendas.* Madrid: M. Ginesta.
1879 *Mittheilungen aus dem Escurial.* Tübingen: Bibliothek des Literarischen Vereins in
Stuttgart, 141.
Köhler, Reinhold
1900 *Kleinere Schriften.* 3 vols. Weimar: E. Felber.
Krikmann, Arvo
1985 "Some Additional Aspects of Semantic Indefiniteness of Proverbs." *Proverbium*
2:58–85.
Kugel, James
1981 *The Idea of Biblical Poetry: Parallelism and Its History.* New Haven: Yale University
Press.
Kuusi, Matti
1972a *Towards an International Type-System of Proverbs.* Helsinki: *FF Communications*
211.
1972b Reprinted in *Proverbium* 19:699–735.
La Rochefoucauld
1976 *Réflexions ou sentences et maximes morales.* Edited by Jean Lafond. Paris: Gallimard.
Lévi-Strauss, Claude
1983 *Le Regard éloigné.* Paris: Plon.
Libro de Alexandre
1934 Edited by R. S. Willis. Elliott Monographs in the Romance Languages and
Literatures, no. 32. Princeton: Princeton University Press, and Paris: Presses Universi-
taires de France.
Libro de Alixandre
1982 Edited by Dana A. Nelson. Madrid: Gredos.
Libro de Apolonio
1976 Edited by Manuel Alvar. 3 vols. Madrid: Castalia/Fundación Juan March.
Libro de los buenos proverbios

1879 Edited by Hermann Knust. *Mittheilungen aus dem Escurial.* Tübingen: Literarischer Verein, 1–65.

Libro de los cien capítulos
1960 Edited by Agapito Rey. Indiana University Humanities Series, no. 44. Bloomington: Indiana University Press.

Libro de los exenplos por a. b. c.
1941 Edited by John E. Keller. Madrid: CSIC.

Libro del caballero Zifar
1982 Edited by Joaquín González Muela. Madrid: Castalia.

Libro del cauallero Çifar
1984 Edited by Marilyn Olsen. Madison: Hispanic Seminary of Medieval Studies.

El Libro del cauallero Zifar
1929 Edited by Charles Philip Wagner. Ann Arbor: University of Michigan Press.

Loader, J. A.
1986 *Ecclesiastes: A Practical Commentary.* Grand Rapids, Mich.: Eerdmans.

Lucanor. See Juan Manuel.

Maimonides [Moses ben Maimon]
1956 *Guide for the Perplexed.* Translated by M. Friedländer. 2d edition. Boston: Dover.

Malbim [Meir Loeb ben Jehiel Michael]
Commentary on the Torah (in Hebrew). Printed in standard editions of the Hebrew Bible with commentaries.

McKane, William
1970 *Proverbs: A New Approach.* Old Testament Library. London: SCM.

Menachem ha-Meiri
1969 *Perush 'al Sefer Mishlei* [Commentary on the Book of Proverbs]. Edited by Menachem Mendel Zahav. Jerusalem: Otsar ha-Poskim.

Merkle, Karl
1921 *Die Sittensprüche der Philosophen "Kitab Adab al-Falasifa" von Honein Ibn Ishaq.* Leipzig: Harrassowitz.

Mieder, Wolfgang
1985 "Popular Views of the Proverb." *Proverbium* 2:109–43.

Mieder, Wolfgang, and Alan Dundes (editors)
1981 *The Wisdom of Many: Essays on the Proverb.* New York: Garland.

Milner, George B.
1969a "De l'Armature des locutions proverbiales: essai de taxonomie sémantique." *L'Homme* 9:49–70.
1969b "Quadripartite Structures." *Proverbium* 14:379–83.
1969c "What Is a Proverb?" *New Society* 332:199–202.
1971 "The Quartered Shield." In *Social Anthropology and Language.* Edited by E. Ardener. London: Tavistock, 243–69.

Mishnah
1932 Edited and translated by Herbert Danby. Oxford: Clarendon.

Murphy, Roland E.
1981 *Wisdom Literature. The Forms of Old Testament Literature.* Vol. 13. Grand Rapids, Mich.: Eerdmans.

The New Oxford Annotated Bible: Revised Standard Version
1977 New York: Oxford University Press.

Ochs, Peter (editor)
1990 *Understanding the Rabbinic Mind: Essays on the Hermeneutic of Max Kadushin.* Atlanta, Ga.: Scholars.

O'Kane, Eleanor S.
1950　"On the Name of the refrán." *Hispanic Review* 18:1–14.
1959　*Refranes y frases proverbiales españoles de la edad media.* Anejo del *Boletín de la Real Academia Española.* Vol. 2. Madrid: Real Academia Española.
Parker, A. A.
1981　"The Humour of Spanish Proverbs." In Mieder and Dundes 1981:257–74. Originally published as *The Humour of Spanish Proverbs.* London: Hispanic and Luso-Brazilian Councils, 1963, 3–23.
Patte, Daniel
1976　*What Is Structural Exegesis?* Philadelphia: Fortress.
1990a　*The Religious Dimension of Biblical Texts.* Atlanta, Ga.: Scholars.
1990b　*Structural Exegesis for New Testament Critics.* Minneapolis: Fortress.
Patte, Daniel, and Aline Patte
1978　*Structural Exegesis: From Theory to Practice.* Philadelphia: Fortress.
Permyakov, G. L.
1979　*From Proverb to Folktale. Notes on the General Theory of Cliché.* Translated by Y. N. Filippov. Moscow: Nauka.
Perry, T. A.
1987a　"Juan Manuel's 'Ystoria deste Exienplo.' " *Romance Notes* 27:89–93.
1987b　*The Moral Proverbs of Santob de Carrión.* Princeton: Princeton University Press.
1987c　"Quadripartite Wisdom Sayings and the Structure of Proverbs." *Proverbium* 4:187–210.
1993　*Dialogues with Kohelet.* University Park: The Pennsylvania State University Press.
See also Santob de Carrión.
Petrus Alfonsi
1911　*Disciplina Clericalis.* Edited by A. Hilka. Heidelberg: Carl Winter.
Pirkei Abot [Ethics of the Fathers]
1932　In Mishnah.
Plessner, M.
1954–55　"Remarks on the *Musrei ha-Filosofim* of Hunayn ibn Ishaak and Its Hebrew Translation" (in Hebrew). *Tarbiz* 24:60–72.
Plutarch, *Moralia*
1970　"De Garrulitate." Translated by W. C. Helmbold. Loeb edition, vol 6. Cambridge: Harvard University Press.
Poema de Fernán González
1981　Edited by Juan Victorio. Madrid: Cátedra.
Rad, Gerhard von
1972　*Wisdom in Israel.* London: SCM.
Revised Standard Version (Bible). *See* New Oxford Bible 1977.
Rosenthal, F.
1940　"On the Knowledge of Plato's Philosophy in the Islamic World." *Islamic Culture* 14:387–422; 15:396–98.
Roth, W.
1965　*Numerical Sayings in the Old Testament. Vetus Testamentum,* supplement no. 13. Leiden: Brill.
Rothstein, Robert
1968　"The Poetics of Proverbs." In *Studies Presented to Professor Roman Jakobson by His Students.* Edited by Charles E. Gribble. Cambridge, Mass.: Slavica, 265–74.
Russo, Joseph

1983 "The Poetics of the Ancient Greek Proverb." *Journal of Folklore Research* 20:121–30.
Sánchez de Vercial
1961 *Libro de los exenplos.* Edited by John E. Keller. Madrid: CSIC.
Santob de Carrión
1947 *Proverbios morales.* Edited by I. González Llubera. Cambridge: Cambridge University Press.
1986 *Proverbios morales.* Edited by T. A. Perry. Madison: Hispanic Seminary of Medieval Studies.
Saussure, Ferdinand de
1959 *Course in General Linguistics.* Translated by Wade Baskin. New York: Philosophical Library.
Scott, C. T.
1976 "On Defining the Riddle: The Problem of a Structural Unit." In *Folklore Genres.* Edited by D. Ben-Amos. Austin: University of Texas Press, 77–90.
Scott, Robert B. Y.
1965 Proverbs, Ecclesiastes. Anchor Bible, 18. New York: Doubleday.
1976 "Folk Proverbs of the Ancient Near East." In Crenshaw 1976:417–26. (Originally published in *Transactions of the Royal Society of Canada* 55, ser. 3 [June 1961]: 47–56)
Segal, Moshe Tsvi (editor)
1964 *Sefer Ben Sira' ha-shalem.* Jerusalem: Bialik.
Seitel, Peter
1969 "Proverbs: A Social Use of Metaphor." *Genre* 2:143–61.
Stein, Ludwig
1900 *Untersuchungen über die "Proverbios morales."* Berlin: Mayer & Müller.
Sturken, Tracy
1974 *Don Juan Manuel.* New York: Twayne.
Sturm, Harlan
1969 "*The Conde Lucanor:* the First Ejemplo." *Modern Language Notes* 84:286–92.
1970 *The Libro de los buenos proverbios: A Critical Edition.* Lexington: University of Kentucky Press.
Suard, François, and Claude Buridant (editors)
1984 *Richesse du proverbe.* 2 vols. Lille: Université de Lille III, Travaux et Recherches.
Tanakh: The Holy Scriptures.
1988 The New JPS Translation According to the Traditional Hebrew Text. Philadelphia: Jewish Publication Society.
Taylor, Archer
1931 *The Proverb and an Index to the Proverb.* Hatboro, Pa.: Folklore Associates.
Taylor, Barry Paul
1983 "Juan Manuel, El Conde Lucanor, Parts II–IV: Edition, Stylistic Analysis, Literary Context." Ph.D. dissertation, University of London, King's College.
Thompson, John Mark
1974 *The Form and Function of Proverbs in Ancient Israel.* The Hague and Paris: Mouton.
Thompson, Stith
1955–58 *Motif-Index of Folk Literature.* 6 vols. Bloomington: Indiana University Press.
Todorov, Tzvetan
1970 *Introduction à la littérature fantastique.* Paris: Seuil.
Twain, Mark
1982 *The Adventures of Tom Sawyer.* Edited by Guy Cardwell. New York: Library of America. (Originally published 1876)

Van Leeuwen, Raymond C.
  1988   *Context and Meaning in Proverbs 25–27.* Atlanta, Ga.: Scholars.
  1990   "Liminality and Worldview in Proverbs 1–9." In *Paraenesis: Act and Form.* Edited by Leo G. Perdue and John G. Gammie. Semeia 50. Atlanta, Ga.: Scholars, 111–44.
Walsh, John K.
  1976   "Versiones peninsulares del *Kitab adab al-falasifa* de Hunayn ibn Ishaq: Hacia una reconstrucción del Libro de los buenos proverbios." *Al-Andalus: Revista de las Escuelas de Estudios Arabes de Madrid y Granada* 41:355–84.
Walther, Hans
  1963–67   *Proverbia Sententiaeque Latinitatis Medii Aevi.* Göttingen: Vandenhoek und Ruprecht.
Waugh, L.
  1980   "The Poetic Function and the Nature of Language." *Poetics Today* 2/1a:57–82.
Westermann, C.
  1971   "Weisheit im Sprichwort." In *Schalom, Festschrift für A. Jepsen,* Arbeiten zur Theologie 1:46. Stuttgart:73–85.
Whiting, B. J.
  1931   "The Origin of the Proverb." *Harvard Studies and Notes in Philology and Literature* 13:47–80.
Whybray, R. N.
  1974   *The Intellectual Tradition in the Old Testament.* Berlin: de Gruyter.
Williams, James G.
  1981   *Those Who Ponder Proverbs: Aphoristic Thinking and Biblical Literature.* Sheffield: Almond.
Wünsche, August
  1911, 1912   "Die Zahlensprüche in Talmud und Midrasch." *Zeitschrift der Deutschen Morgenländischen Gesellschaft* 65:57–100; 66:414–59.
Yee, Gale A.
  1989   " 'I Have Perfumed My Bed with Myrrh': The Foreign Woman in Proverbs 1–9." *JSOT* 43:53–68.
Zakovitch, Yair
  1977   "The Pattern of the Numerical Sequence Three–Four in the Bible," Ph.D. dissertation, Hebrew University (in Hebrew with English summary).
Zimmerli, Walther
  1933   "Zur Struktur der alttestamentlichen Weisheit." *Zeitschrift für die alttestamentliche Wissenschaft* 10:177–204. Reprinted in English translation in Crenshaw 1976:175–206. Translated by Brian W. Kovaks.

GENERAL INDEX

INDEX OF BIBLICAL REFERENCES

INDEX OF NONBIBLICAL WISDOM
AND OTHER CLASSICAL TEXTS